BEADS!

BEADS!

Make your own unique jewellery

•

STEFANY TOMALIN

David & Charles

Stefany Tomalin, a founder member of the Bead Society of Great Britain, runs the Necklace Maker Workshop in Portobello Road, London, a treasure trove of antique and unusual beads from all over the world. She researches, exhibits and lectures in both UK and USA, and has written numerous features, articles and reviews for popular and specialist craft publications, and is working on her third bead book.

Photographs by Jeremy Finlay
Illustrations by Gerald Larn

A DAVID & CHARLES BOOK

First published 1988
Reprinted 1989, 1991, 1992, 1993, 1994, 1995

A catalogue record for this book is available from the British Library.

ISBN 0 7153 9838 5

Typeset by ABM Typographics Ltd, Hull
and printed in Hong Kong
by Wing King Tong Co. Ltd
for David & Charles
Brunel House   Newton Abbot   Devon

FOREWORD

Beads have been greatly beloved through the ages, forming as they do the basic ingredients of our popular and costume jewellery. They are endlessly adaptable, as they may be repeatedly rearranged and rethreaded to suit the colour schemes of the moment. The different colours, patterns, shapes and textures of individual beads create intriguing possibilities; perhaps a style as intimate and personal as a hair-style or favourite pair of shoes, or wildly extravagant and sensational.

My first beads were inherited; later, I found cheap treasures in antique markets or swapped with friends. The interest grew, and I discovered that the history and archaeology of beads were as under-researched as the neglected techniques of making and threading beads. I had studied the basics of jewellery and silversmithing, but it seemed that threading beads was for primary school or occupational therapy, definitely not for serious designers!

This led to experimentation – mixing unexpected materials, colours, patterns, and sizes; sometimes even working out techniques to include cords and knots as an additional decorative element. From repair work, exhibiting, teaching, and selling loose beads, I also discovered the wide interest in the subject, from serious students, to people just wishing to keep their own beads repaired, or thread up a boxful of broken necklaces for a charity bazaar.

At the present moment there seem to be more jewellers than ever designing and making beautiful and innovative pieces, often using alternative materials in preference to the traditional precious metals. Craftspeople are experimenting with all sorts of miniature and small-scale techniques; collectors and the fashion-conscious are starting to re-evaluate what used to be dismissed as 'costume' jewellery, and the hand-made beads of stone, ceramic and glass of 'early' or 'primitive' peoples are being appreciated and worn alongside conventional jewellery. Indeed trends are broadening to include colour, pattern and light as well as weight, texture, movement, and so on. Relative values of materials have changed too: while stones like garnet or freshwater pearls are more plentiful and cheaper than ever, true red Mediterranean coral gets scarcer and more expensive as accessible sources are fished out; and substances such as new ivory and tortoiseshell have strict import restrictions.

Glass as a precious material is increasing in value as resources dwindle, or require expensive man-hours to produce. Hand-made glass, whose quality is the result of a lifelong skill and hours of attentive work, is in greater demand than ever. At the other end of the scale, specialist manufacturing techniques are now able to produce in quantity the polished stone beads that were once the achievement of the experienced human hand and eye alone.

It is still surprising that although more agate, quartz and jasper beads are being imported from the Far East and India than ever before, too often they are poorly threaded, often on breakable cotton or unpleasantly stiff and brittle nylon fishing line. Restringing is scarcely better from your average high-street jeweller; even if silk is used, it is often disfigured with blobs of glue. However, it is a fairly simple matter to restring your own beads, as there are very few difficult techniques to master and the end result will be more satisfying and professional. That in itself is sufficient reason to justify this simple, factual and comprehensive book of instructions!

So the aim is to gather into one volume what I looked for from the sixties onwards and didn't find: a descriptive collector's guide, with advice to help distinguish the various semi-precious stones, types of glass etc; how certain beads can be made by hand; every useful and possible method of threading, including 'beadwork' (textile techniques with beads), beads on wire (earrings in particular); plus mending and tips on restoring. There are hints on the practical elements of designing with beads, and, finally, a useful reference section.

It is a privilege to be able to write about a subject that I really love, that I naturally long to share the skills, ideas and fascination with as many people as possible, and to feel that the research has been informative and entertaining for whoever may become interested by this book. A warning, however: beads can quickly become addictive!

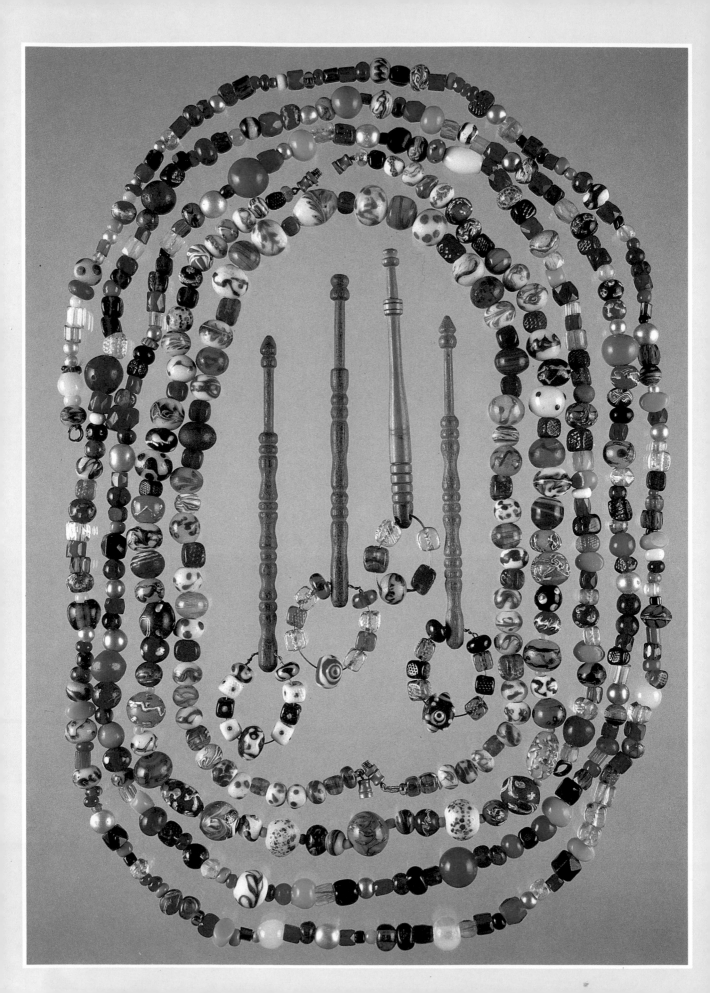

CONTENTS

Collection of English lace-bobbin spangle beads.
All these beads were originally on bobbins like the ones in the centre (one antique with its original glass beads, three with glass beads handmade by Henry Spooner in traditional patterns). Although they resemble Venetian glass beads, they have consistent styles of their own, and may have been made as a sideline to other glass work in Britain in the eighteenth century and onwards, to be sold at markets and fairs with newly made bobbins

INTRODUCTION

Why do human beings still derive pleasure from handling and wearing beads? Their origins, materials, techniques and design contribute to their value, but something else is stirred. There is excitement, wonder, admiration; the inexpressible associations of copper and gold, pearl and jet, coral and turquoise, amber and lapis, opal, jade, ruby or emerald – these are more than just the labels of mineral and other substances. A sort of enchanted power is kindled by these names; treasures straight out of fables and legends, perhaps? Or the accessories that define and express human beauty, wealth, and love?

Beads are a particularly accessible and versatile form of adornment, and, next to body painting, surely the oldest. A bead is anything with a hole through it, a decorative or symbolic component to be threaded, usually with other beads, in a sequence – random, processional, or approximately symmetrical.

They were most precious and magic to me as a little girl – owner of an inherited collection kept in a George VI coronation cake tin. Most of them were old hand-made Venetian glass beads, all subtle glowing colours. They were decorated with swirls, rosebuds and trailed designs that looked like calligraphy; others pearly or sparkly. There were also coral twigs and tiny pierced tropical seashells with a shimmering rainbow lustre.

Whatever it is about beads that attracts children joyfully or collectors ardently and seriously, it seems to belong to all cultures, as beads feature in many myths, traditions and rituals around the world. There was the necklace called Brisingamen for which the Norse goddess Freya lay on successive nights with each of the four dwarves who fashioned it; and the jewelled girdle symbolising virginity in the medieval French tapestries of the Lady and the Unicorn. Effigies of deities and saints bedecked with necklaces, jewels and other votive offerings can be seen in many religious shrines. The Inca kings threw their gold and jewels into Lake Guatavita to propitiate their gods. Carved Nigerian twin idols are decked out with necklaces each year. The Babylonian goddess Ishtar, looking for her lover Tammuz in the Underworld, was able to pass through the seven gates only by taking off a piece of jewellery at each one. Pharaohs such as Ahknaten honoured their élite with gifts of beaded collar-necklaces. From Homeric Greece to Ancient China and Tibet, beads were symbolic and precious.

From some of the earliest discovered stone age burials we know that as well as using their ingenuity to make tools, our ancestors were adorning themselves with teeth, claws, bones, seeds, nuts, shells and small fossils with natural holes. Before the appearance of metalworking skills, the men and women who chipped flint were also able to pierce or bore holes in natural substances and the softer stones, attaching them by means of hair, grasses and sinews to decorate their bodies. The drilling was by no means easy, yet the beads must have been prized enough to justify probably hours of work to create one small hole – and their perforations were fine and exact. Perhaps we may assume that, just like us, those wearers appreciated the intrinsic beauty and charm of their beads simply as adornment, and, just like us, they probably also saw them as lucky charms, keepsakes, the regalia of power and rank, magic amulets or religious talismans, birthstones, signs of wealth, marks of identity, family, betrothal and other allegiances.

Moreover, because the harder beads are virtually indestructible, they can continue to circulate indefinitely, being repeatedly rethreaded according to the whim and fancy of their successive owners. By changing hands this way they reappear right across the trade routes of the old and new worlds.

Unfortunately, there is still a kind of false discrimination which denigrates beads as the least important, commonplace, primitive or childish type of jewellery. The insurance premium on beads is lower than silver and gold. They are nearly always considered different from real jewellery ('Can I wear them with my good ear rings?'). The fact that they are on thread seems to imply that bead necklaces are temporary or unsafe, but an individually designed, properly threaded and knotted bead necklace is almost certainly stronger than a gold chain from a high-street jeweller – and possibly more unique, extravagant and valuable. Beads can of course be extremely cheap and still be special and attractive without being in imitation of anything else. Your range of ideas with beads may be broadened as you try out some of the techniques in the following chapters.

IDENTIFYING BEADS

This section contains some basic guidelines to help you distinguish the materials and origins of old beads. It is, however, only a general summary, and the reader is recommended to consult more specialised reference books (see Bibliography) for more detailed information. Gemmology can be studied for a special diploma of the Gemmological Association of Great Britain, or the Gemmological Institute of America.

If you inherit a string, or a boxful of loose beads, or hunt in bric-à-brac, jumble, or charity shops, this chapter is likely to be useful, as enormous quantities of old beads of all kinds are to be found in antique markets. It is a practical safeguard, however, to double-check. Even honest dealers may not be gemmologists, and occasionally you may find valuable beads dismissed as plastic. So it is well worth while to 'train yourself up'.

The very earliest beads that sometimes appear on the market here or abroad may be described as 'ancient Egyptian mummy beads', 'tomb beads' 'Roman glass', 'Pre-Columbian', or 'Islamic', none of which terms by itself is particularly precise historically or geographically. Recently strung ancient beads very often contain a mixture. I have picked up strings of glass of the Roman period in New York, Jerusalem and the Birmingham Rag Market!

Anything up to the sixties is considered collectable, and plenty of the glass and plastic beads available today were already being manufactured twenty-five years ago or more, as the same beads frequently appeared in those copious multistrand necklaces that went with cloche hats and huge earclips covered with 'petals'. These necklaces still turn up in jumble sales and Oxfam shops.

First, establish if the beads are stone, glass, metal, pottery, an organic substance, or plastic.

STONE OR GLASS?

Stone and glass are often difficult to distinguish. They are both similarly hard, cold, smooth and usually shiny, and both can be transparent, translucent or opaque. Glass can be deliberately made to imitate stone in various ways – with streaks, flecks and blotches. The most perfect of gemstones are cut and used in settings. Clear gemstone beads are usually made from the offcuts or parts of the crystal with variations, strata or so-called flaws. Gemstones differ from glass in these ways: members of the quartz family may have visible strata inside them; beads cut from solid crystals will show the stratified layers across the form, independent of the bead shape, as they are cut from larger fragments of stone. Their holes are made by drilling, usually from each end, hopefully to meet in the middle – where the bead is transparent it is usually easy to see where they meet. (Bad drilling is more often seen on cheap recent imports from India.)

Glass beads that may be confused with gemstones are often made by the 'winding' or 'lampwork' technique, or even moulded – they are sometimes cut with facets afterwards. A wound glass bead will have a spiral structure, often of slight colour variations, and seldom without bubbles, even if they are so minute that you need to use a magnifying glass. The hole will be straight, and often coated with a chalky powder. Some clear glass beads are treated to give an internal 'crackle' effect which also closely resembles the flaws in quartz. A wound or moulded glass bead afterwards cut into a faceted shape may still have a small rounded surface at each end where the hole is, a cut gemstone will have the hole starting and finishing sharply in flat facets at the ends.

The term 'crystal' can mean the natural colourless gemstone quartz, or fine quality cut glass.

Opaque glass will not allow you to look for flaws, but if it seems to resemble a gemstone it may have the traces of spiral winding. It may also have had a peppering of coloured or metallic flecks melted on the outside in imitation of the texture of jade, lapis or aventurine quartz, for example. If it were broken, this would immediately be obvious.

PRECIOUS AND SEMI-PRECIOUS STONES

The following table lists precious and semi-precious stones and associated precious substances by colour (opaque or transparent). The most well known in each category are shown in capitals.

	Opaque	**Transparent**
Red	CORNELIAN, CORAL, Jasper, Bloodstone, Heliotrope, Sard	RUBY, GARNET, Tourmaline, Rubellite
Pink	Rhodocrosite, Rhodonite, Botswana Agate, Angelskin Coral	ROSE QUARTZ, Tourmaline, Rubellite
Purple	Lavender Jasper, Porphyry, Chalcedony	AMETHYST, Fluorite (Blue John)
Blue	LAPIS LAZULI, Sodalite, Blue Aventurine, Blue Lace Agate, Labradorite, 'Swiss Lapis', stained Agate	SAPPHIRE, Iolite, Tourmaline
Turquoise	TURQUOISE, Crysocolla (Eilat stone), Australian Opal, Odontolite stained Howlite ('Turquorite'), Amazonite, Utahlite, Plasma	AQUAMARINE
Green	JADE, MALACHITE, Jasper, Opal, Aventurine Quartz, Jadeite, Nephrite, Bowenite, Moss Agate, Amazonite, Aragonite, Bloodstone, Chrysoprase, Unakite, Plasma, Prase, Onyx Marble, Serpentine ('Connemara Marble')	EMERALD, PERIDOT, Olivine, Chrysolite, Verdite, Tourmaline
Yellow	AGATE, AMBER, Sunstone, Steatite (Soapstone), Alabaster (Gypsum), Onyx Marble, Aragonite, Bowenite, Jade	TOPAZ, AMBER, Citrine, Rutilated Quartz, Orthoclase, Feldspar
Brown	AGATE, JASPER, TIGER'S EYE, Cornelian, Alabaster, Banded Agate, Bauxite, Marble, Steatite, Fossilised Wood, Sardonyx, Bowenite, Jade, Meerschaum, Granite, Serpentine, Hawk's Eye	TOPAZ, AMBER, Citrine, Almandine, Garnet
Grey	LACE AGATE, Howlite, Haematite, Marcasite, Zebra Agate, Turitella Agate, Fossil Coral, Botswana Agate, Pyrite, Serpentine, Jasper	SMOKY QUARTZ, Rutilated Quartz, Geode
Black	ONYX, JET, Banded Agate, Obsidian, Granite, Flint, Jasper, Lava, Haematite, Serpentine, Black Coral	
White	LACE AGATE, MOONSTONE, PEARL, OPAL, Gypsum, Satin Spar, Talc, Steatite, Calcite (Chalk), Alabaster (Gypsum), Howlite, Mother-of-Pearl, Meerschaum, White Coral, Marble, Ivory	QUARTZ ('CRYSTAL')

The names of the well-known materials are often mis-applied. If in doubt, consult one of the reference books on gemstones, and consider the alternatives of similar colour. You will soon get to know the main characteristics and the differences. There follows a few notes about some of the most well-known stones, etc, as these are specially useful when relating to beads.

Of the dozen or so traditional precious stones, **diamond, zircon** and **spinel** are not drilled into beads, to my knowledge. **Ruby, emerald** and **sapphire** are, though only the rather interesting non-transparent turbid parts of the stone. Sometimes these are made to sound more important by names like 'root of emerald', or 'ruby matrix'. As their value is in their carat weight, the holes are deliberately as small as possible. **Aquamarine, topaz** and all the beautiful and varied colours of **tourmaline,** mostly mined in Brazil these days, are made into all sorts of shapes as

Gemstones.
From top: antique bracelet with emeralds, rubies, sapphires, and turquoise beads.
String of assorted tourmalines.
Topaz aquamarine and opal chips.
Fourth string, from left: tiger's-eye, amber from African jewellery, Baltic amber, citrines, garnets, large jasper, cornelian, corals.
Loop, clockwise from centre top: jade and aventurine pendants, moss agate, bloodstone, smoky quartz, large pale agate oval, lace agate, ivory, rose quartz, amethyst, natural dark banded agate, jet beads including Victorian carved jet, carved stained vegetable ivory, lapis lazuli, five different natural turquoise beads, malachite, jade.
Within: four pendants of carved jade, jasper, rose quartz. Victorian seed pearl choker, and various baroque and fresh-water pearls

beads – the offcuts are also tumble-polished, drilled and strung as baroque gemstone necklaces. Often, stones are cut into beads somewhere quite different from their place of origin; emeralds are found in Columbia, Brazil, Zimbabwe, the Transvaal, Zambia, Tanzania, India, Pakistan, Australia and the US, but every string of emerald beads I have ever seen has been shaped and drilled in India. Emeralds and rubies feature particularly in the lavish jewellery of the Moghuls. Various stones from all over the world are also shipped to Idar-Oberstein in West Germany where there is an established traditional gemstone industry.

Opal is something of a rarity in beads, but can be really pretty and mysterious, with its flashes of light.

Turquoise is a popular but expensive stone, so there are a variety of substitutes, imitations and simulations. Natural turquoise is rather porous and tends to get darker and greener. Modern turquoise is nearly always 'stabilised', impregnated with a protective resin which may be tinted. Chippings of the real stone are bonded together to make reconstituted turquoise; **turquorite** is a natural, creamy-white stone called **howlite** which is stained a turquoise colour, and sometimes used nowadays in North American Navaho Indian jewellery. **Odontolite** is supposed to be fossilised bones buried near copper deposits which have somehow absorbed the colour from the copper oxides, etc in the soil. Small fragments of this, embedded in a black resinous composition are used like inlays, in some traditional Islamic jewellery.

Real **jade** is actually two of the toughest, hardest stones, **nephrite** and **jadeite,** both often variegated in colour. **Jadeite** may be paler and marbly, **nephrite** more flecked in appearance. Both come in creamy, paler and brilliant darker greens, reddy-browns to black, and never transparent. Both are quite valuable and sometimes large items such as solid bangles and pendants are carved. Indian jade is actually aventurine quartz, a natural green stone with tiny glittery speckles throughout. Goldstone glass is sometimes called aventurine glass, to add to the confusion. The **jades** should be distinguished from **amazonite,** and **serpentine,** which is much softer. Some beads and Chinese carved pendants are made of a softer stone called **bowenite,** sometimes a creamy-green or brown. The Chinese also cunningly imitate jade with glass.

Swiss lapis often occurs in Victorian necklaces, but it is in fact a grey-beige **jasper,** stained with a cobalt or Prussian blue. It does have a mellow appearance, unlike the stained agates, whose blues, greens and hard blacks always remain rather artificial looking.

For ivory, amber, pearl, coral and jet, see Organic Materials (page 13).

The whole subject of imitation stone beads is a fascinating one, and would make the theme for a specialised collection in itself.

POTTERY OR CERAMIC BEADS

Unglazed biscuit-fired terracotta-type pottery beads are easy to recognize and made in many countries. Some cheap Peruvian ones are decorated with ordinary paint which rubs off quickly, making them more suitable for earrings than necklaces. Many types of ceramic beads have been made: from the real ancient Egyptian mummy beads to the delicately glazed and minutely decorated Chinese porcelain; interesting freely modelled coloured porcelain beads, hand made in this country by potters, sometimes with two colours marbled together unglazed; or ceramic beads from Greece with transfers added; also every imaginable lustre, glaze, etc. Of particular interest to collectors are large 'maiolica' beads made up to the 1920s in Gubbio and Deruta in Italy, decorated with pious Latin mottoes, intended as corner weights for linen altar cloths.

Faience beads

Faience, or Egyptian paste, is a type of ceramic paste containing its own colour and glaze which works in one firing. Such beads were made in enormous quantities in Pharaonic Egypt, particularly the seventeenth to nineteenth dynasties (approximately 1700–1200BC), the earlier ones being more intense in colour and less breakable. The colours are strong blue, turquoise blue, green, brown, black, and ochre yellow to cream. There are exquisite collars of these beads in many shapes in the British Museum and Victoria and Albert Museum. The cylindrical ones were also threaded, honeycomb fashion, into bead net 'aprons' placed over the fronts of mummified bodies. Despite their age, so many of these dainty beads were made that plenty of them turn up in markets at affordable prices, rethreaded into single loops. The formula has been rediscovered and they are widely imitated, but the copies I have seen are rough and crude, and larger. (A similar recipe is used today in the Middle East to make large turquoise blue beads worn by donkeys to keep away evil spirits.) Predominant shapes in ancient Egypt were little cylindrical tubes, rings or discs and sometimes double rings like a figure of eight used as spacers, spheres and small amulets, but the collars included leaves, flowers, fruit and insect shapes. The tubes were made with a very liquid mixture – strands of grass were dipped into it then cut into lengths and dried, the grass burned away during firing. The brightest, most vivid turquoise blue beads are finer, stronger, and also more valued. Other motifs and flat shapes were produced in quantity in shallow moulds.

See the recipe in Chapter 7 on p72.

METAL BEADS

All types of metal beads are also made in many countries. Silver coloured beads from the Third World may be called 'silver', but generally the constituents of the alloy, although possibly including fine silver, are not in the correct proportions to deserve the British hallmark, and it is therefore illegal to describe it as 'silver'. The term 'native silver' may be used. Some ethnic metal beads with a yellowish tinge may be predominantly nickel. In Ethiopia, the old traders' Portuguese silver coinage was melted down and used for their beautiful Coptic Cross pendants, other jewellery and long strings of small beads. Many native silver beads today come from India, and are more correctly described as traditional folk jewellery rather than as antique, because they are still being made.

A popular type of bead is now fashioned in India with the metal thinly plated onto a resin core. Many are made by stamping sheet metal into a shaped mould, then soldering two matching halves together. A typical Islamic shape is the 'collared' bead, with a collar or strip around the hole at each end. The Ashanti of West Africa make bronze and gold beads, casting by the 'lost wax' method. Chinese craftsmen manufacture delightfully delicate genuine silver or silver gilt wire filigree beads, decorated fasteners and other jewellery, and many intricate 'cloisonné' enamel beads.

'Rolled gold' or 'goldfilled' is a modern substitute made with some fine gold and retains some of its qualities, such as resistance to tarnishing, but is tough and cheaper. Sometimes it looks pinkish.

There are now methods of putting a very thin metallic coating on plastic which looks authentic if a bit shiny, known as vacuum plating.

People with allergic tendencies to certain metals may find that gold, surgical steel, sterling silver or even rolled gold will avoid the problem.

ORGANIC MATERIALS

Most organic materials are easy to identify, with only a few exceptions.

Ivory

In the days of the British Empire, craftsmen in the Dominions produced all sorts of fine and exquisite carving, with the Chinese and Indians working in particular in ivory, using bone as a cheaper alternative. Supplies of elephant or walrus ivory must have been scarce and expensive, but monkey or camel bone is too coarse for detailed work. The Chinese and Japanese started to use another substitute called vegetable ivory. This is the hardened kernel of a Central American palm nut, which resembles ivory and could be stained and carved in a very similar way. Ivory has an almost translucent 'grain' of fine layers that looks like even, curved crosshatching; old ivory jewellery may absorb sweat and grease, and get slightly yellower, and old ivory beads sometimes develop hairline cracks along the grain, where dirt may collect. Bone is rougher, pitted along the grain, and it can also be stained and will yellow. The roughness and its more splintery nature make it more difficult to carve and polish finely. Vegetable ivory has a visible grain similar to ivory but has a tendency to crack, if anything across, not along the grain. Some items from India are now carved of reconstituted bone, which appears to have no grain at all, but has a definite smell of scorching if burned, like ivory and bone, which confirms that it is not plastic. Strings of Buddhist prayer beads from Nepal and Tibet carved in the form of tiny skulls are a reminder of mortality. These were made of human bone in the past, though modern examples are now of camel bone.

Amber, ambroid, horn

A great deal of well-documented research has been done on amber, and there are complex chemical analytical tests which will alone determine if it is amber beyond any doubt. However, there are these three rules-of-thumb to help you in the market-place: real natural precious amber is not a mineral, but the resin from certain trees that has been preserved or fossilised in sedimentary layers for billions of years. It is transparent or opaque in every shade and tint of yellow, greenish-brown, and orange towards deep brown. Sometimes small insects or twigs are entirely embedded in it, which add to its value. Most of it comes from the Baltic coast area, some from Sicily, Burma and recently the Dominican Republic.

Testing for genuine amber is easier if you use unthreaded beads. Real amber is extremely light, it shatters easily and is inflammable, and it will sink in water but float in brine (saturated salt solution). If you scrape a tiny amount with a penknife in a place where it cannot show, next to the hole, it should yield tiny splinters; if it throws up a shaving it is not amber. Look closely to see if someone else has already tried this test, then you may not need to damage it yourself. Thirdly, the heat test: touch the inside edge of the hole with a heated needle or pinpoint, and smell it, for amber has a resinous incense-like fragrance, whereas plastic gives off acrid fumes. The method of trying to pick up tiny pieces of paper by attraction is not a good test, as many plastics have static electrical properties. Old necklaces of real amber may have original screw fasteners of amber to match, although matching plastic ones are now also made.

Amber chippings can be recycled by being melted down and pressed by a patented Victorian process. This reconstituted substance is called 'ambroid' which is not so breakable as amber and can be recognised by strata in it resembling cirrus clouds. Pipe stems are often made of ambroid.

Copal resin is another natural substitute for amber chiefly from Zanzibar. Much of the African 'amber' jewellery made with the opaque yellow variety is much more likely to be copal, which may show cracks. Raw natural resin can also be pressed and shaped when partly congealed.

Plastic amber-coloured beads are often also old and can be quite pretty in the right context. Necklaces that resemble amber are nearly always very expensive but that is no guarantee of their authenticity. Although less popular, the transparent amber is actually more valuable, especially if it has inclusions or insects trapped inside. The large opaque mustard yellows that are used in Bedouin, Tibetan and North African necklaces are also often other substances, but as long as the price is not astronomical it shouldn't matter too much because they do look spectacular.

Horn beads can bear a resemblance to golden and brownish opaque amber, but when heated or burned, horn has an unmistakable scorching smell.

Tortoiseshell
Tortoiseshell is sometimes a constituent of Victorian jewellery. It is easy to shape if immersed in hot to boiling water for a few minutes, and left to cool in its new form. It is most attractive in thin layers to let the light through the natural variegated pattern. However, the hawksbill turtle from which it is obtained, under cruel conditions, is now an endangered species, and imports into Britain and the USA are strictly controlled.

Jet
Jet is fossilised coal, not too brittle to be lightly carved, and weighs less than glass or stone. Popularised by Queen Victoria when mourning the death of Prince Albert, the best examples came from Whitby on the Yorkshire coast but jet of inferior quality had to be imported from Spain when demand increased, and this tends to crack and break more easily. Jet is too brittle to make into very small beads. All the 5mm (¼in) and smaller black faceted embroidery beads

on clothing are glass. To imitate jet, black glass beads were sometimes made hollow by blowing into a mould so they would seem lighter. The old black faceted glass beads are often called French jet. Ebony and black 'bog oak', both dense dark woods, are sometimes confused with jet, although it is not difficult to see the grain of the wood. Another Victorian patented substitute for jet was vulcanite or ebonite processed rubber. I have never seen beads but only pendants of this. Testing with a hot needle would yield a typical burning rubber smell.

Shell and mother-of-pearl
Mother-of-pearl is quite distinctive, being a thick pearly lustrous white shell carved into various bead shapes and is a favourite for rosaries. It can also be stained. Satin spar or moonstone may be mistaken for it. Abalone (paui shell) is similar but grey with a multicoloured lustre. Parts of other species of shells are sometimes made into beads, the orangey-pink cameo shell in the south of Italy seems very like the pink 'angelskin' coral, and the most prized North American Indian 'wampum'-pipe shaped beads were made of white or bluey-purple shell. Various white shells have been carved and used since ancient times such as the misleadingly named hippo tooth, and also the ostrich egg shell and land snail shell made into discs in Africa.

Coral
When first fished out of the sea, coral is still easily pierced, which may explain why it sometimes has incredibly tiny holes. It is quite possible that a great deal of the coral in Tibetan, North African and Nigerian necklaces and regalia comes from the Mediterranean. The deep red coral is the most highly prized and becoming scarcer as the shallow waters are overfished, so the colour is sometimes artificially enhanced. Recently, 'apple coral' has appeared in many necklaces. This comes from the Philippines, and is a different variety but similar to sponge coral, which is highly porous and may be given almost any colour. The beads are saturated with clear or tinted synthetic resin which protects them and makes the substance durable although it could be said that its nature it totally altered. Golden or black coral is different again, rather woody or like horn, or even hardened treacle toffee. I have seen necklaces of it in twig shapes. Twig or branch coral of any colour is less valued than the round beads, especially if they are a good size.

Ancient beads. Egyptian faience mummy beads and amulets. 'Roman glass', possibly from Iran, including eye beads

APPROXIMATE CHRONOLOGICAL CHART OF BEADS TO AD1700

	EUROPE and MEDITERRANEAN	RUSSIA and NEAR EAST	AFRICA
100,000 BC Neanderthal Man			
30,000 BC Late Palaeolithic Aurignacian	FRANCE collars including fossil crinoid, animal teeth and bone beads BRITAIN pierced wolves' teeth CZECHOSLOVAKIA fossilised shell necklaces and stone beads	Sungir, RUSSIA, mammoth ivory beads	
21,000 BC	SPAIN amber beads		
10,000 BC		ISRAEL shell and bone beads TURKEY softer stone and copper beads	LIBYA shell beads
7000 BC	YUGOSLAVIA softer stone beads CYPRUS and CRETE cornelian and shell beads	SYRIA stone and shell beads	
5000 BC Bronze Age		IRAQ stone bead shapes MESOPOTAMIA cylinder seals, gold and stone beads	
3400 BC		IRAN gold beads etched and shaped stone beads found at UR SYRIA faience	EGYPT shell, stone, glazed steatite NUBIA faience
3000 BC	BALTIC amber trading GREECE silver beads CRETE gold and faience beads	CAUCASUS, Russian, glass beads	
			EGYPT early dynastic period glass beads, faience and beadwork
2400 BC		TROY granulated gold MESOPOTAMIA glass beads	12th dynasty onwards (including Akhenaten and Tutenkhamun) elaborate faience collars, prolific production of faience and glass components. Eye beads
2000 BC	BRITAIN jet beads made and traded Aldbourne WILTS and Rillaton CORNWALL amber stone and bone faience and bronze beads Stockbridge, HANTS, calcite, jet, lignite faience and shell beads Folkton, YORKS, decorated bone beads Melfort Argyle, SCOTLAND, complete complex jet collar Upton Lovell, WILTS, Baltic amber and gold beads CRETE granulation techniques (Minoan era)		
1000 BC	MYCENAE gemstone beads, amber, faience trading	TURKEY elaborately shaped gold and silver beads	
600 BC	CELTS made glass beads PHOENICIA complex molten glass techniques, face beads. Trading	IRAN and areas under Roman rule, production of 'Roman glass' beads	ALEXANDRIA Ptolemaic Egypt 30–304 BC 'mosaic glass' beads N. Africa area 'Roman glass' beads
200 BC Roman Empire	BRITAIN Sutton Hoo Anglo-Saxon treasure including beads		
AD 200		RUSSIA stone glass and shell beads BYZANTINE glass beads	
AD 600	VIKINGS chequered millefiori and wound glass beads SCANDINAVIA glass beads being made	'ISLAMIC' styles of glass and stone beads ISRAEL Jerusalem glass beads	
AD 1000	and in CENTRAL EUROPE, MEKOVINGIANS etc.		
AD 1100	ITALY Venice glass industry established, kept secret		NIGERIA glass beads
AD 1200	GERMANY Idar Oberstein Agate beads industry begins		CAIRO bead trade centre
AD1291		Marco Polo describes eastern craftsmanship	
AD1254 to 1324	Venetian secrets escape to Holland, Bohemia, Germany, Spain. Glass industries established making beads		
AD1600	World exploration, merchant trading beginning, creating enormous demands for beads for barter.		
AD1700	Gablonz BOHEMIA glass bead production expanding Founded by runaway Venetians, becomes increasingly important manufacturing centre		AFRICA European and Indian beads brought in for barter

ASIA	NEW WORLD
INDIA shell beads	
KOREA, CHINA and JAPAN stone, teeth, bone and shell beads	
MONGOLIA shell and fossil beads	AUSTRALIA kangaroo bone beads
INDIA/PAKISTAN softer stone beads	
	MEXICO shell beads
TURKESTAN bone, shell, stone, turquoise and clay beads	NEVADA shell beads
KOREA jade beads THAILAND shell and stone	
INDIA etched cornelian and many stone beads produced	MEXICO stone beads
AFGHANISTAN etched cornelian	N. AMERICA copper beads
INDIA, CHINA, JAPAN glass beads	MEXICO and PERU crystal and jadeite beads
INDIA Cambay etc stone beads trading west into Africa, east and north into Asia, also glass 'trade wind' beads	
NEPAL gold and silver beads THAILAND glass beads	
TIBET etched agate 'dzi' beads	PERU Inca and Chimu shell, stones, crystal, turquoise, etc.
CHINA Marco Polo describes Buddhist rosaries	intricate shapes
1644 onwards CHINA Canton glass bead production	N. and S. AMERICA European beads brought in

Pearls

Even the amateur can easily distinguish real pearls from fake, or simulated pearls, whatever the size or shape, by rubbing gently against a tooth. The artificial coatings on imitation pearls are completely smooth, the real thing will be slightly rough and gives a hard grating sensation. Also, rather surprisingly, real pearls seem heavier than glass. But even experts may disagree as to whether a pearl is wild and natural or cultured (grown on a pearl farm). Any roughly shaped pearls are called baroque, and the small irregular rice-grain-sized freshwater pearls from Japan and China, that look like pearly grubs or mouse droppings, are sometimes tinted. They are also known as river pearls or Biwa pearls, as they are cultivated in Lake Biwa in Japan. In recent years they have become steadily cheaper. The most valuable have the best iridescent lustre and are not too wrinkled-looking. Seed pearls are the tiniest round creamy-white pearls, often irregular, used in quantity in oriental jewellery. They come from the stretch of sea between India and Sri Lanka. Beautiful delicate necklaces were made with clusters of seed pearls attached to templates of mother-of-pearl shell to resemble garlands and bunches. The pearls were stitched on with very fine gut. Some of these Victorian necklaces survive but many are now in need of major repairs, and it is not easy to match up missing ones.

Wood

Woods commonly carved into beads are distinguishable by their colours, grain and sometimes fragrance, including among others ebony, beech, mahogany, rosewood, laburnum, boxwood, padauk, olive wood, pine, sandalwood, bamboo and cork. Wooden beads can often be found carved with the typical raised circle and dot pattern on rosaries or necklaces. The pattern is made easily with a revolving tool that cuts the shallow circular grooves rather like a compass drawing a circle, repeated around the circumference of the bead.

Pips, seeds and nuts, sometimes elaborately carved, and a few interesting extras such as teeth and claws, complete the list of organic-material beads.

MODELLED AND PLASTIC BEADS

Modelled substances, both self-coloured and painted, include resins, gesso, lacquer, pasta, papier maché, papier roulé, rose petal paste, sealing wax, cinnabar and myrrh, and there are wooden beads from the twenties encrusted with tiny round glass 'hundreds and thousands'. Some collectors specialise in art deco, in which case they may have found plenty of interesting pieces including chrome and plastic, and faceted and moulded glass from Czechoslovakia. Many designs were geometric and abstract, but the Tutankhamun and oriental themes, fashionable at that time, appear too.

Early plastics include celluloid, bakelite, casein and vulcanite. Perspex, acetate and coloured cast resins are more recent, and the collection might need to include some of the 'pop-it' beads of the fifties and sixties. All these mass produced, throwaway ornaments may have very little material value, and yet their design and style are characteristic of the epoch, making them collectable. (In other cases it is the individual beads which make a necklace valuable, which usually means that you can rearrange and recombine beads without detracting from their value.)

GLASS BEADS

Glass has been and still is the most versatile of all the materials of which beads are made, with an amazing range of colours, patterns, textures and forms made by endlessly varied methods over the centuries by skilled craftspeople. Glass is, of course, not only transparent and colourless but has many vivid clear colours, milky or translucent, and also completely opaque (inaccurately called chalk, china or porcelain).

If you are just starting a collection of beads you may feel safer sticking to the well-known and recognisable gemstones, but as you observe and learn more it is likely that the variety of glass beads will become increasingly fascinating. Most of the cheaper glass beads are made in moulds. It is usually evident because there will be a giveaway seam line around the bead, either along the 'equator' or 'through the poles'. Sometimes there will be a small ridge where the two halves of the mould join, whereas sometimes it has been smoothed away and only a slight difference in colour or transparency is visible.

While writing this book a man came into my shop to look at the beads. He hardly spoke any English but we managed to converse in German. He told me he had been a political prisoner in Czechoslovakia, and his release had been negotiated by some influential individuals in Britain and he was here to thank them. He explained that he had been in a prison near Jablonec, the glass industry centre in Czechoslovakia, where he had to work making moulded glass beads all day. This was the work of all the inmates of that prison, one hundred men, of whom eight were, like him, prisoners of conscience. He described in detail the processes involved in the heating, moulding, piercing

while molten, polishing and smoothing of the beads, and in some cases cutting facets. I understood that fasteners were also assembled and plated in that prison, and that one man is expected to produce around ten thousand beads per day or six hundred thousand bolt ring fasteners. Factories for moulded glass beads have been set up by people from Jablonec in Germany and Austria. Iridescent faceted crystal beads called Aurora Borealis are a typical product from a company called Swarovsky now located in Austria.

Recycling glass
In parts of the tribal areas of Ghana and Nigeria, short or long cylindrical powder glass beads are made using ground up coloured glass fused in open stone or clay moulds sometimes in horizontal striped layers or with longitudinal stripes against a plain ground. The look is attractive, rough and ancient, and a most appropriate way to recycle European medicine or beer bottles or broken beads.

Glass-blowing
Some glass-blowing techniques are not so difficult to adapt to a smaller scale for bead making. The Venetians and the Chinese have made beads which are in fact a bubble with two holes, sometimes blown into a shaped mould to imitate jet, for instance. The beads are sometimes made clear or coated on the inside with paint, mirror-silvering (like Christmas tree baubles) or a pearly substance. Another method is to blow a large bubble of glass, which is stretched when molten and pulled out to form a long thin tube. Simple glass beads of all colours can be made in quantity from short segments of the tubing, finished off by heating a second time in a rotating drum to melt the surface smooth. The great majority of small glass embroidery beads (rocailles and the longer bugles) were made this way at least as far back as AD1000. Somewhere on the coast of the island of St Agnes in the Scillies is a beach with a rock pool known as Beady Pool, because a ship with a cargo of small red-brown seed beads made this way was wrecked nearby in the last century,

Selection of the widest possible variety of lampwork glass bead shapes and colours.
The second-longest strand shows various beads with precious metal foil embedded as a reflective layer under transparent colour. Next inwards are all hollow shapes, some blown, some built up. The blue oval has paint on the inside surface. The short curved strand has hand-made beads by Henry Spooner. The centre strand is of hand-made glass beads including hand-made millefiori flowers, by Douglas Ledger

and the beads turn up among the pebbles and shells of the low-water line along the shore.

Sometimes the original glass tubing had coloured stripes added to its length, or a star or rosette pattern was created in cross-section with three or four layers of different colours. If the ends of each bead were bevelled or rounded, the pattern showed as a zig-zag like a sharpened pencil. Made in Venice and later Holland, these 'chevron' beads were very highly prized Venetian trade beads in Africa; they were also used for trade with the Crow Indians and others of North America.

Lampwork

The most amazing variety of types of glass beads, however, are variations of lampwork. Working at a bench with a blowtorch, gas jet or other controllable source of intense heat and using glass in the form of rods or canes of plain or patterned glass, the two hands are free to manipulate the molten ends of the canes in the flame with a tool, like the makers of glass animals in seaside towns. The base of these spirally wound beads is a blob formed around a mandrel – a revolving metal rod usually coated to prevent sticking which is slid out when the glass begins to cool and harden. Mandrel-wound beads can be made as small as 3mm (⅛in) diameter up to 40mm (1½in) but at that size even if the holes are quite large, the beads are still very heavy. The best size-graduated glass bead necklaces are of beads made in this way by hand. In the winding process, bubbles are trapped in the glass and can be seen inside in the typical spiral form. In the molten state, the possible decorative variations are endless: apart from being made of plain or coloured mixtures of glass, a textured or patterned surface can be added by sprinkling on crumbs of glass of another colour (they melt on to resemble brown sugar over a hot rice pudding), or metal filings, or slices of millefiori patterned canes. The bead can be pressed against a tool to produce a ribbed or waffle surface, or pinched or pressed into a different shape, known as 'marvering', and trailed decoration can be applied with coloured glass canes – almost like drawing, writing or cake icing in the hands of a skilled craftsperson.

These techniques are found particularly in early Roman and Viking glass, in India, Venice, Czechoslovakia, China, Japan, Holland, Hebron and Nigeria.

IDENTIFYING BY THREADING MATERIALS

Beads as necklaces can be further categorised by style, threading materials and fastenings. Some old hand-made glass, crystal or stone bead necklaces are strung on a fine silver chain called foxtail, with the ends actually soldered onto the rings of the fastener, thus proving that the beads are valuable. Unfortunately clear beads tend to accumulate a black layer of tarnish on the insides of the holes which looks like dirt and obstinately refuses to be scraped out. Decorated Venetian glass beads, graduated in size with small matching hand-made beads in between, were often threaded without a fastener into a long continuous over-the-head loop. Indian necklaces of precious gemstone beads often favoured the adjustable sliding Turk's head knot, with a tassel at the end and gold or silver threads braided into the cords.

Rosaries or prayer beads require a certain number of beads with intervals or stoppers. The Chinese Mandarin necklaces were based on Tibetan prayer beads, which were a long string of round beads with four very large ones, often of precious stones or substances resembling them. One of the stones would have a T-shaped perforation so that a balustrade bead and a tassel could be attached, while some also had three extra dangling cords with additional beads and tassels.

Recently I acquired some old beads from amongst a collection of haberdashery items. They were made of wood and entirely wound round with silk strands, and came in several colours as well as white and cream. They were recognised by an elderly customer who used to work in a trimmings factory who told me these were often used to make tastefully trimmed upholstered satin coffin linings – a survival of some ancient burial custom perhaps?

2
THREADING MATERIALS, TOOLS AND EQUIPMENT

Part of the beauty of a necklace of threaded beads is that the whole thing hangs without tension, gracefully emphasising the movement of the wearer, and subtly drawing attention to face, eyes, hair, neck or bosom. The method of threading can accentuate or ruin that effect. When properly threaded the beads are safe and protected from damaging each other, and they articulate freely in their chosen sequence.

THREADS

Threading material will need to fulfil as well as possible these requirements: load-bearing or breaking strength; resistance to abrasion and fraying; flexibility and 'knotworthiness'; slowness to deteriorate; resistance to stretching; looking good. The choice of an appropriate thread will depend mostly on the sizes of the smallest holes in the beads. If the beads have large holes almost anything can be used. If the chosen material is thick enough the strength will be adequate, but with very small-holed or precious beads it will be necessary to consider maximum strength in relation to thickness. Very fine thread can easily be used doubled once or several times because of the need for strength, and if the holes in the beads are filled by thread it will protect them, preventing their moving too much from side to side and grinding against each other and besides, the necklace looks better when the beads are well aligned.

Of course, there is an enormous variety of possible threads. No doubt the earliest necklaces were hung on fibrous grasses, animal sinews or hair, and were repeatedly restrung. These fibres are still used; I have bought beads from Africa recently, strung on raffia, and on skeins of cotton waste, and also have repaired fine coral beads and seed pearls that had been strung on horsehair.

Natural fibres
Leather thong, so long as it is reliable, supple enough and not likely to crack, is easy to thread, and comes in 1m (1yd) lengths or spliced on a continuous reel.

There are also other kinds of fat, strong, natural or synthetic sinew or gut.

The largest-holed beads can also look good on any kind of ornamental cord. Haberdashery or furnishing trimming departments in large stores offer a choice of colours and designs, and interesting combinations of simple fibres can be made into cord by plaiting, twisting, using a knitting dolly, finger-knitting, etc. The Japanese have a traditional technique of braiding called *kumihimo* which is worth investigating. See the Bibliography for Catherine Martin's book on the subject. A cord will be simpler to thread if you can stiffen the end with a little cylinder of sellotape or a coating of nail varnish or wax. When rigid, the end can be cut into more of a point so it pushes through easily. After threading, the end can be trimmed off, and perhaps unravelled to make a tassel.

Horsehair has now been superseded by fishing line or nylon monofilament gut which is available in a great range of thicknesses. I only use it to try out designs, as it is a lazy, unsatisfactory way of threading. The stiffness makes it tempting because it needs no needle, but it is very difficult to knot and finish off neatly, it doesn't hang properly, it stretches and goes brittle and tends to break without warning. Being springy, it will send beads flying off in all directions at a high velocity!

Of the natural fibres, silk is the strongest in relation to its volume. It comes in a range of beautiful colours or can be dyed, and has been traditionally used for precious beads. Silk stretches and shrinks less than linen or cotton.

Linen carpet or button thread is very tough and hard-wearing but not so attractive. Cotton is slightly weaker than linen but comes in many colours and will blend with clothing, and is available everywhere.

All these organic fibres, however, have a limited lifespan. They should not be wet too often. Under ideal conditions, such as undisturbed in caves in the Judaean desert, they may survive many centuries, but with normal wear and tear they begin to perish, usually next to the fastener first. In the past it was a matter of routine to get the ancestral pearls re-threaded regularly, generally before any major social or ceremonial event at which they will be required to be worn. Nowadays even if you can find a good pearl stringer, the cost will be considerable. Some jewellery firms who do valuations and insurance will insist on rethreading the pearls first.

Synthetic fibres

These have been developed for increased strength, and have various patent names. Polyester, terylene and rayon sewing threads are as tough in equivalent thickness as most of the organic threads, but are brittle, which means they may fray easily or snap suddenly under strain. Kevlar is the brand name of another newly developed fibre which is also extremely strong, as with nylon thread, but it is very expensive. Used for example in archery for stringing bows, its particular quality and advantage over nylon thread is that it will not stretch. Sports shops sell it in large reels.

Wire is used to thread beads for earrings or small links, in a more or less rigid context (see Chapter 5), but for a hanging necklace a continuous wire is not recommended because with repeated bending and flexing it will become brittle. Some of the Czech glass bead necklaces are on a twisted steel cable, which is very difficult to knot satisfactorily and will kink, is not rustproof, and if it unravels it is prickly.

Another new threading material which is intended to combine the strength of nine-strand steel cable with a smooth nylon outer coating is called tigertail. With a very high breaking strength it is easy to thread up, being stiff it doesn't need a needle and can be attached to a fastener using a crimps or callottes (see pages 33-6). Its drawbacks are that it is stiff and springy so it won't hang loosely, therefore it is best used for short chokers which is rather a waste of its strength, and it kinks. Once folded you will be landed with a necklace with an ugly corner in the middle of it, which won't unkink. It is, however, useful for bracelets, and is available from craft suppliers and fishing tackle shops.

Beads are sometimes threaded on thin rope-like chain called foxtail, or other fine chain. If the chain is made of solid, closed links, it will be quite strong. The chain is attached to fastener loops with a small ring called a jump ring.

Elastic such as hat elastic or shirring elastic makes necklaces of light beads which stretch to go over the head and need no fastener. This can also apply to bracelets, and black jet pieces, often double drilled, are quite suitably threaded as bracelets on elastic.

Dental floss is unspun polyester fibre, preferably waxed, which will pass through fine holes but is rather hard to knot tidily. Spun nylon thread (bonded, siliconised or waxed) is by far the most versatile and strongest flexible spun thread. It is only available from specialist suppliers. There are all colours and thicknesses from 40 (normally three ply), 60 (two ply), to 80 which is extremely fine, though not always easy to obtain. Nylon thread is made from continuous smooth filaments twisted together. This makes it relatively more slippery, less likely to fray and easier to tighten knots accurately. Many strands can be combined and used together for bulk or to create an interesting colour mix, or in an emergency the plys of 40 can be separated by unravelling into two or three finer strands. When a final knot has been made on a necklace with the nylon and the extra threads cut off close to the knot, the whiskers can be sealed to prevent any unravelling or loosening of the knot by passing a lit match across them (see page 32). It will melt and shrink the ends into a minute blob just above the knot, like sealing wax.

Builder's line, kite string, surgical suture, even velvet ribbons may be to hand and worth experimenting with. Whatever the fibre, nylon is the only one that melts as described. For a beginner, a reel of 40 white nylon thread is a must, as it can even be used in conjunction with embroidery cottons to give strength in a knotted necklace while the coloured cotton provides the bulk and the visual ingredient to the knots.

Glass beads, even the tiny rocailles, are made with standard sized holes, and normally 40 or 60 thread doubled will easily fit. Much smaller holes are encountered in coral and small pearls, and some of the smallest precious stone beads worked in India will need 60 or 80. Occasionally the old thread may get jammed inside a bead. Very useful tools can be obtained called broachers. They are sometimes sold in a set of sizes, and are a long fine tapered steel spike with a sharp triangular cross-section. You push it through and twiddle it to clear and enlarge a hole, but it is not a drill and is fragile.

NEEDLES

Rigid steel 'beading needles' are sold in sizes 10–15, the higher numbers being finer, and are easier to find in assorted packs. They have their uses but they also have some real disadvantages. Beading needles have an elongated slit-shaped hole to take thread of a

Necklace of agate geode slices, moonstone beads, chips of opal, and embroidery beads. It is constructed with a second small pendant at the centre back, so if the necklace is looped round twice, the pendants dangle one above the other at the front

reasonable volume of filaments which may be coaxed through by fanning them out. Try it – you may have the aptitude; no needle threader is fine enough to do it for you. The inner edges of the needle's eye are also likely to cut the thread if you have to strain to pull it through all the beads, and if you break the needle you will have the difficult choice between starting again or knotting in a new double thread which may show. A beading needle will suffer if you tackle cheap drilled gemstone beads with crooked holes; it may well end up curved or bent, and you will find its useful life limited. There is no alternative to the needle when working patterns with embroidery beads and bead weaving (see Chapter 6), where a number of regular small beads have to be threaded through more than once; also in combination with leather, cloth, or soft seeds which a needle will easily pierce. (When it comes to throwing these needles away, stick them into a cork or match-box or bundle them up with sticky tape, as the ends are lethally sharp and the eyes sometimes fracture into a nasty barb that can harpoon itself into an unsuspecting finger.)

For straight threading, you could get some mileage out of a flexible nylon dental-floss threader, but it may not be very useful as it is fairly fat.

The most useful all-round needle must surely be the home-made one made of very fine soft wire, about 8cm (3¼in) long, doubled, and the 2.5cm (1in) at the ends twisted together. Some fine wire is too springy and brittle to twist, but 3 or 5 amp fuse wire, or the copper strands from unravelled electrical cable are ideal for all but the very finest work. Your spoiled bits of gimp (see page 36) will uncoil into an even thinner strand which will work with the 80 thread for the tiniest corals and pearls, though it may often need re-placing as you go along. The advantages of these home-made wire needles are: they are easy and cheap to make; easy to thread as you can make the eye as large as you need; they are easily replaced even in mid-project; they are far less likely to damage the thread or the beads; being flexible they go round all necessary corners; they are not dangerous; they are as thin as regular needles; and they allow for any special knot for finishing, as the needle can be removed at the end without cutting the thread (see page 37).

WORKING AREA

Before starting, prepare your work area, preferably in a dust-free room without other furniture, and a smooth, seamless floor – at least no deep-pile carpet nor heavy wardrobes with gaps underneath. Your de-sign may simply be a row of repeated beads or a set graduated in size, or an imaginative arrangement, which will need initially to be spread out in front of you so that the beads do not roll away. Traditionally, pearl stringers work on a surface with a piece of velvet on which to set out the beads, but chunky corduroy or elephant cord provides ready-made grooves that help stop the beads joggling out of sequence. Double-sided tape, thinly rolled pastry, children's soft model-ling compounds or Blu-tack are also useful. If your velvet is on a tray it will be easier to lift it out of the way without disturbing the contents. Your small beads should be poured into solid shallow dishes – ashtrays are good, plastic yoghurt pots are hopeless as they are tall, light and tip easily.

Store your beads in clear, lidded containers such as jam pots. Exposed beads get very dusty but you need to be able to see what you have as raw materials for the next design.

NECKLACE LENGTHS

A single strand choker for an adult should be approxi-mately 40cm (16in).
45cm (18in) (princess) fits inside an open-neck blouse
65cm (26in) (matinée) is unflattering to the larger bosom
Up to 60cm (24in) will need a fastener, anything over that length will go over the head without undoing
80cm (32in) with a fastener will go twice around the neck
90cm (36in) (opera)
Over 90cm (36in) (sautoir, muffchain or charleston length)
120cm (48in) with fastener will go three times around, anything longer than that could be dangerous – if hanging straight it hangs below waist level and catches on doorknobs etc. although it can look ex-tremely elegant
A bracelet is approximately 18cm (7in) (half a choker length)
Number of regular beads, depending on beads' diameter per 40cm (16in) choker length:
3mm (⅛in) 133, 4mm (⁵⁄₃₂in) 100, 5mm (⅕in) 80, 6mm (¼in) 66, 8mm (⁵⁄₁₆in) 50, 10mm (²⁄₅in) 40, 12mm (½in) 33, 15mm (³⁄₅in) 27, 20mm (⁴⁄₅in) 20, etc.

When thread lengths are given in the methods, it always means the length of *doubled* thread. A generous extra amount should be allowed for finish-ing knots.

You may feel best able to design freely by laying out the beads on the surface in front of you. If a size-graduated or other symmetrical design is intended, start with the centre bead then work up each side by putting down the other components in pairs. When

ESSENTIAL TOOLS

model maker's
hand-held electric drill

hand-made fuse-wire needle

beading
needles

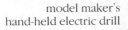
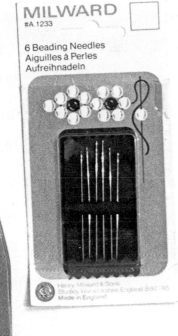

set of broachers

Swiss
watchmaker's
tweezers

darning needle

tambour hook
in handle

small sharp
manicure scissors

round-nosed pliers
(coarser and finer)

snipe-nosed pliers
(with flat inner surfaces)

fine wire cutters

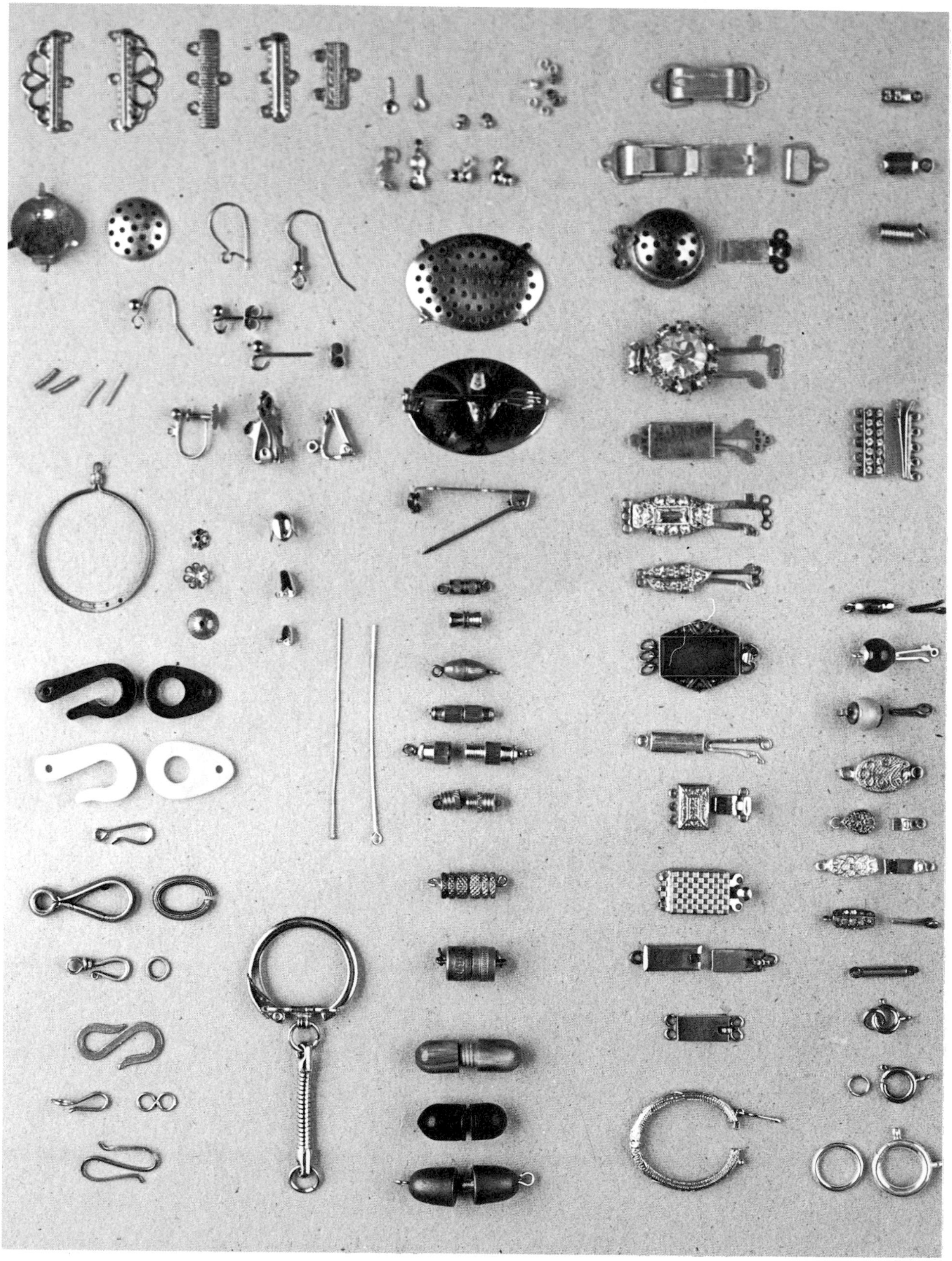

FINDINGS

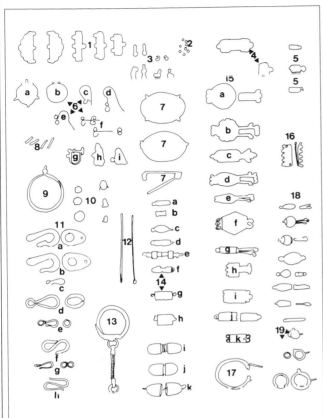

1 End spacers
2 Crimping beads (French crimps)
3 Callottes (lower right) and similar types of end crimps or necklet ends
4 'Hinge' bracelet snap (open end closed)
5 Crimps for leather thong or thick cord

6 Earrings fastenings:
   A, B clip with template for bead decoration
   C kidney wire
   D fish hook
   E ball and loop (shepherd's crook)
   F ball and loop stud with butterfly clip
   G earring screw for non-pierced ears
   H, I clips with loops for non-pierced ears
7 An oval brooch back and template, plus bar-pin brooch back
8 Cut lengths of bullion, gimp or purl, ready for use
9 Hoop with row of holes for dangling earrings
10 Assorted filigree and smooth bead cups or bell caps
11 Hook fasteners for necklaces
   A horn
   B bone
   C metal wire
   D spring hook with loop (antique)
   E handmade Indian silver
   F hammered brass 'S' hook
   G rolled gold (goldfill) hook and loop
   H rolled gold (goldfill) wire 'S' hook
12 Head pin and eye pin
13 Key ring blank
14 Screw clasps, with and without loops: A-H metal; I horn; J wood; K metalised plastic
15 Push snap fasteners:
   A multistrand with template for bead decoration
   B F various types of multistrand 'fishhook' safety snaps, some set with imitation stones
   G single-strand 'fishhook' safety snap
   H and I cheapest mass-produced multistrand box snaps
   J and K nickel-plated box snaps from India
16 Unusual antique multistrand snap fastener set with faceted stones
17 Necklace shortener or twister clasp
18 Single-strand push snap fasteners
19 Bolt rings with split ring, jump ring or ring soldered shut

your idea is clear, thread temporarily onto a thread securely knotted into a loose loop which you can then try on and play with, or hang up and look at objectively. Once satisfied, you will be able to follow through with the most appropriate threading method.

SUMMARY OF ESSENTIAL TOOLS

These lists are a handy reference for tools needed, and most are discussed fully in the sections describing their use.

Making beads
Small precision modelmaker's drill, twist drills of sizes 0.5–2mm, 4mm for holes for leather thong, diamond drill bits and assorted burrs
Set of broachers, preferably with detachable handle or to be held in a pin vice
Set of needle files
Scalpel or craft knife
Knitting needles, cocktail sticks, plasticine
Stone tumbler

Threading
Small sewing scissors, curved nail scissors, old kitchen scissors
Swiss watchmaker's tweezers, tapering to an exact fine point

Scalpel or craft knife	Matches
Set of broachers	Beeswax
Darning needle	5 amp fuse wire

Beadwork
Beading needles (size 10 or assorted 10 to 15)
Bead loom (bought or home-made)
Tambour hook and embroidery frame

Working with wire
Pliers: round-nosed, snipe-nosed with smooth jaws, chainlink or rosary pliers which include wire cutters
Fine wire cutters

Cleaning beads
Jam jar half full of potato starch	Silver dip
	Old nylon socks
Soft old toothbrush	Soft cloths
Pure soap	

Generally useful
Magnifying lens (not hand-held, to leave the hands free)
Assorted glass screw-top jam jars, and small dishes or trays (heavy, preferably not plastic) for storage, sorting and working.

FINDINGS

This is the trade term for a range of ready-made mass-produced metal components used as attachments and fastenings to assemble a piece of jewellery. They are normally made of inexpensive plated metals but can be sterling silver, rolled gold (goldfill) or gold (9 carat, 18 carat or 22 carat). Clasps may be set with real or imitation stones. Earring wires must be chosen carefully to avoid allergic reactions: surgical steel or high-carat gold are usually safest. The findings listed below are particularly suitable for use with beads.

Necklaces and bracelets
FOR ATTACHING THREAD TO FASTENER:
    Callottes
    Crimps (French crimps, cramping beads)
    Leather crimps
    Folding crimps
    Bullion (gimp, purl, French wire, necklet ends)
SNAP FASTENERS:
    Box snap, push snap, cylinder snap, multistrand snap, safety snap, fish-hook snap, hinged bracelet snap
SCREW FASTENERS:
    Barrel clasp, torpedo screw clasp, also available made of amber, bone, ivory, horn or wood to match beads
OTHER FASTENERS:
Bolt ring plus split ring or jump ring	Swivel clasp
	Spring catch
Hook and eye	Necklace shortener
S-hook	(twister clasp)

ADDITIONAL NECKLACE FINDINGS:
Bead cups (plain or filigree)	End spacer
	Chain
Spacer bar	Necklet tag

Earring findings:
Ear clips	Kidney wire
Ear screws	Ball and loop hook
Ear wires	Fish hook
Sleepers	Head pin
Post and butterfly (or scroll)	Eye pin

Findings for pendants
Bail	Spring bail
Bail and loop	Jump ring
Leaf bail	Bell cap

Other findings
Brooch pin	Perforated template
Brooch back	Key ring

3
STRAIGHT THREADING TECHNIQUES

In Old-time Tools and Toys of Needlework Gertrude Whiting describes a delightful performing parrot encountered in northern India, who was trained to thread a needle and then pick up beads from its trainer's hand and thread them, one by one. The threading operation has never really been difficult, but it is the designing, knotting and finishing that will distinguish the true craftsperson from the parrot!

When teaching small groups of students, I have found that the complicated and more advanced threading methods are not so daunting if they are taken as exercises graded in order of difficulty, with each one using techniques mastered in the previous stage. For those who like to work independently, adapting the techniques to your own designs as required, it is still recommended that you master the simpler processes first.

Chapter 9 consists of seven complete self-contained projects combining several of these essential techniques to produce pleasing finished work, and wearable pieces of jewellery.

Thread lengths are the length of *doubled* thread. Allow a generous extra amount for finishing knots.

1 THONG CHOKER

Some large-holed beads can be threaded on leather thong, normally 1m (39in) or at least 60cm (24in) long. These chokers work best with 8–13cm (3–5in) of large beads at the front and only smaller beads or bare thong at the sides. When the sequence of beads has been chosen and threaded, hold up the thong by both ends together, letting the beads slide to the centre keeping their position on the thong. Tie a simple overhand knot in the thong at each end of the sequence of beads so that they no longer slide from side to side. The remaining bare thong ends can be used to tie the necklace – if you want to be able to vary the length, leave them long, if it is to be a choker only, then some of the extra thong can be cut off. It fastens with a reef knot, or sliding knot, or sliding within a bead, as explained in Project 1 (see page 82).

Thong choker with overhand knots to secure the beads, and (a) reef knot or adjustable sliding knot (b) to fasten

All kinds of unusual fat cords, laces, braids or tapes can be used in this way, provided the end can be stiffened if necessary with nail varnish or glue for threading. (Types of crimp fastener attachments also exist for thong if the necklace is to remain a fixed length.)

2 SCREW FASTENER

Small screw fasteners are always available with wire loops, and sometimes just with a hole through each end. Ivory, bone and amber necklaces sometimes have matching screw fasteners of this type, or similar. The wire loop is not fixed and is in fact easy to remove in order to thread by this method. It practically

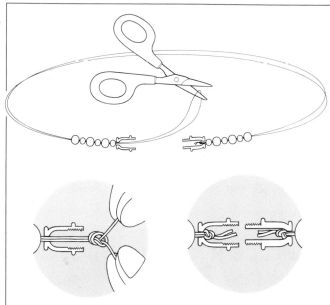

Using a screw fastener. Thread the sequence of beads and remove the needle. Cut the loop and tie an overhand knot to go inside the second half of the fastener, similar to the knot inside the first half at the beginning of the necklace

guarantees a neat finished appearance with the minimum of skill, because the knots are completely concealed inside the fastener.

Using 40 thread double through a wire needle, make an overhand knot securely at the end of your doubled thread, which should be at least 30cm (12in) longer than the total intended length of the necklace. Pick the longer half of your fastener, and thread out from the inside, then thread up your sequence of beads, to the end. Take the remaining flowerpot-shaped half-fastener and thread inwards, through the hole in the bottom. Carefully cut the loop and remove the needle. Now with both strands together, tie another overhand knot. To tighten it down as close as possible to the fastener, start fairly loose, nudge the loose knot closer to the fastener with your fingers, making sure there is no pull on either end, then take the spare threads where they emerge from the knot, separate them and, holding one strand in each hand, pull them away from each other, gradually at first, then really hard. Because the nylon thread is very tough and slippery a knot like this is able to travel a distance without snapping. With practice you will be able to tighten this kind of necklace very effectively. Do not worry if there is a slight amount of slack; when the necklace is fastened and hanging in a loop, the slack is taken up. This is a good neat method for threading inexpensive beads, and you do not have to go through any beads more than once.

NB: If your final knot slides out through the hole in the fastener, do not imagine that it will become a fatter knot if you make a second overhand knot over the first. Either it will result immediately in two small knots close to each other, or you may find that the second knot will slide off later, leaving two small knots. Even the sewing knot, made like an overhand knot with the end through the loop a second time, will result in a knot of the same width but a bit longer and very difficult to tighten accurately, which is also not useful.

If you find this difficult, try using two threads doubled (four thicknesses). It may be safe to use a different type of fastener, although the appearance of a matching screw fastener is visually appropriate with beads of the same material, particularly horn, bone or amber.

3A CONTINUOUS LOOP, AT LEAST 60CM (24IN) WITH NO FASTENER

Using small-holed beads, use 40 nylon thread, doubled, with a wire needle. Never be mean with thread, and allow at least an extra 30cm (12in) to the intended length of doubled thread. Start with a temporary knot at the end of the thread. Thread up your sequence to the end. Undo your temporary knot by pulling the 'tail'. Take both pairs of ends together, tie an overhand knot, tighten as before, cut off close and singe the whiskers. This knot shows, but is not too conspicuous and if singed should be completely secure.

3B CONTINUOUS LOOP WITH TWO SMALL KNOTS

Follow instructions for loop with fastener as far as threading the sequence. If it will go, thread a second time through the first two beads, in the same direction, to close the circle. Cut the end of the thread with the needle and remove the needle. Pull one strand of each pair back out of the two beads ending up with two different pairs of loose ends (rather like changing partners in square dancing). Tie A and C in the first half of a reef knot, then take strand C only, forwards, down and up behind the half-reef knot in the centre. Pull up what slack you can, and where the two strands meet again tie an overhand knot with both strands together as one, and tighten as before by pulling. Pull up the slack and do the same with B and D. The whole

Five art deco 1930s Czech necklaces of faceted glass beads. The outer one was made for the Middle East market

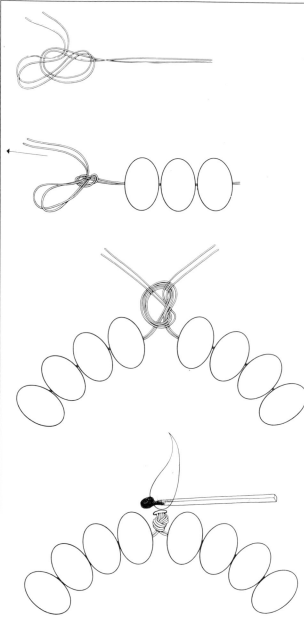

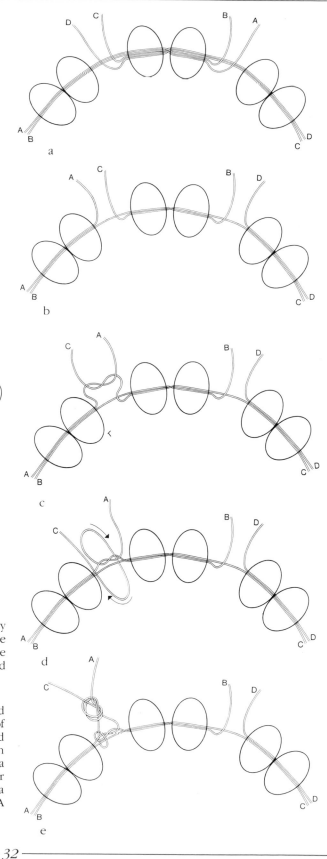

For a continuous loop, using no fastener, tie a temporary knot at the end of the thread. Having threaded the sequence of beads undo the temporary knot by pulling the end of the thread. To join the ends, tie them in an overhand knot and singe the ends

(right)

For a continuous loop with two smaller knots, thread through the first two beads a second time and cut the end of the thread and remove the needle (a). Taking one strand from each of the two doubled threads, pull it back through the two beads (b). Tie strands C and A in the first half of a reef knot (c), and bring strand C towards you, down over strands A and B and back up behind these strands in a clockwise motion (d). Pull up any slack and tie ends C and A in an overhand knot (e).

Tighten by pulling. Repeat with strands B and D

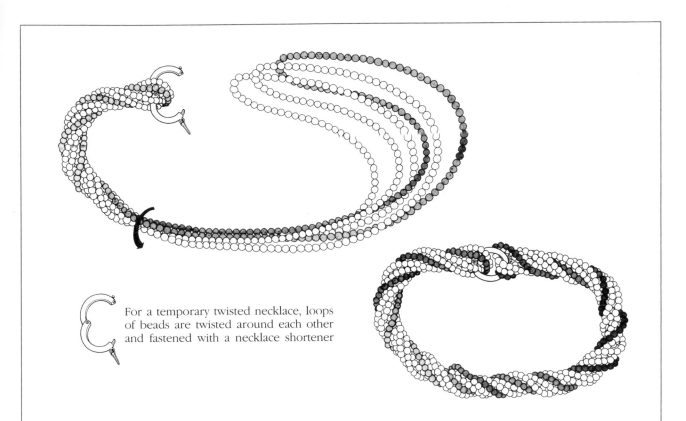

For a temporary twisted necklace, loops of beads are twisted around each other and fastened with a necklace shortener

loop should now be firm and doubly secure, with two independent small knots in two different places. Trim the whiskers and singe. This will leave two very small visible knots instead of one big one. For an invisible join, the knots can probably be slid tightly inside adjacent beads.

Twisting

There is a current trend for taking several equal lengths of 90cm (36in) loops of small beads in harmonising colours (such as pearl, coral and garnet) which can be knotted by the above method, twisting the loops, doubled, around each other and fastening using a loop-shaped fastener sometimes called a necklace shortener or twister clasp.

If you plan this type of necklace, do not make the loops too tight as the twisting needs some extra slack. When the fastener is undone, the twist does not stay. There is a different method for creating a permanently twisted rope necklace, see page 46.

4 CALLOTTES

The majority of available necklace fasteners have loops for attaching the thread. Sometimes the loops are soldered together and sometimes there is a cut so they can be prized open and bent back into place when fixing jump rings or links. The most useful inexpensive type of ring to which a bolt ring can fasten is a 'split ring', like a key-ring. Although it is not soldered there is no easy way that a knotted thread could pull off it. Some fasteners of cheap stamped and folded metal sheet have holes that are just punched and left rough, which tend to cut the threads. All these fasteners can be attached with callottes which are stamped out of metal sheet and come in the form of two tiny cup-shaped hemispheres with an attached ring. They are used by pressing the two rounds together into a small hollow ball shape which encloses and holds a knot in the end of the thread. The attached ring is not soldered shut, and can be inserted through a fastener loop, thus avoiding the use of threading.

It is essential to have at least one pair of small pliers when working with callottes and rings. Round-nosed pliers are specifically designed for opening and closing the small jump rings and links, and a fine-tapered pair with flat, preferably smooth, inner jaws known as snipe-nosed are needed for attaching callottes. Practise by using a bolt ring and split ring with a pair of callottes of the same colour metal. As always the thread should be used doubled at least once with a generous allowance for each end. Make an overhand knot about 15cm (6in) from the end. Thread all your beads and finish by tying another overhand

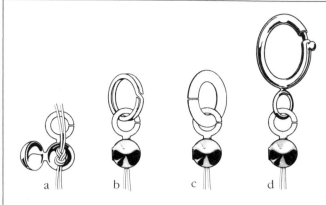

knot after the last bead. Leave the extra 'tails' of thread.

To attach the callottes and fastener, wind the thread tight around your index finger with the knot resting inside the open callotte, with the loop pointing away from the beads. The tight thread holds the callotte in place, while the other hand is free to manipulate the snipe-nosed pliers to press the two halves of the callotte together around the knot. When you are satisfied that it is securely held and will not slip out when pulled, you can cut off the thread ends sticking out of the callotte. Do exactly the same at the other end. A fatter knot such as a figure of eight knot is a bit bulkier and easy to make with practice.

As it won't show, glue could also be added to give the knot bulk inside the callotte and as an additional precaution to prevent it slipping out.

Attaching fasteners with callottes. Tie a knot about 15cm (6in) from the end of the thread and place it inside one half of the open callotte (a). Press the two half-rounds together, enclosing the knot. Callottes can then be connected to: (b) split ring; (c) jump ring; or (d) bolt ring

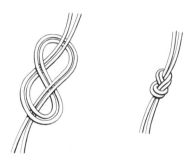

A figure of eight knot is quite bulky but good for going inside callottes. It is easy to make with practice. To complete the knot pass the end through the initial loop and pull to tighten

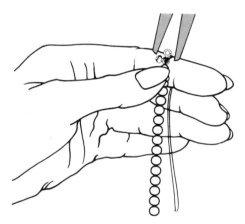

Attaching callottes and fastener to a threaded necklace. Hold the threaded necklace in one hand with the end knot and remaining thread over your index finger, the knot resting inside the open callotte, which will remain in place so long as the thread is pulled tight, while you close the callotte around the knot with snipe-nosed pliers in the other hand

When attaching the loop of the callotte to the fastener loop, as with all open rings, such as jump rings, the ring must be prized open only by twisting the opening apart, using one or two pairs of pliers. If they are not opened in this way the ring is weakened and is very difficult to press together tightly again. When both are attached and bent back smoothly into position, your necklace is complete, with no thread showing, and the fastener and callottes look professional

correct   incorrect

Always open a fastener ring or jump ring by twisting the opening sideways; never make the opening wider. One, or two, pairs of pliers will be useful in the operation

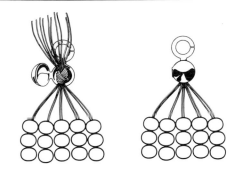

Using many strands knotted together with a pair of callottes

5 CRIMPING BEADS

Crimps or French crimps are either tiny ring-shaped beads or tubes of white or yellow metal. The crimp technique is the best one to finish off short fashion necklaces on fishing line or tiger-tail cable, which is of limited value and should only be used for the shortest necklaces or bracelets, as it does not hang. It is not advisable to use crimps on thread, as they may cut or weaken it.

Choose a fastener with loops, and crimps to match the metal colour. Allow an extra 15cm (6in) at least for finishing. Thread up your design, starting and finishing with a crimp. Take the gut or cable through the fastener loop, then back through the crimping bead and the next one or two beads at each end. Pull it all up close to the fastener ring, and then secure by squeezing hard the metal bead with a pair of snipe-nosed

and neat. You can work fast with this method by stringing up a number of necklaces with somebody else doing the callottes and fasteners, or by stringing a bunch of necklaces first, then completing the fasteners one after the other.

Callottes do not come in precious metals, making them most suitable for inexpensive fashion jewellery, and they will take almost any size of knot. You can work with the ends of several strands knotted together, or you can use a much tougher braid or fine string.

There are some other small fittings similar to callottes, also called 'bead tips' or 'necklet ends' or 'callotte crimps'. These have a small hole through which the thread passes, with a knot concealed inside. They would be threaded rather like the screw-fastener method (page 30) and are limited to thread that would fit the hole. In my experience, the normal callotte is more easily available, more versatile and more reliable.

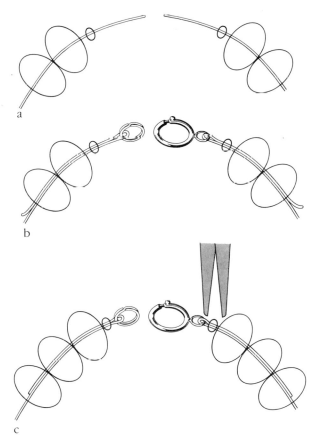

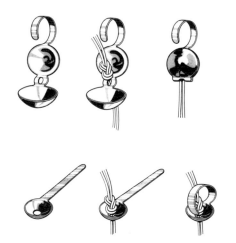

Alternative fittings to callottes – bead tips, necklet ends or callotte crimps. The thread passes through a fine hole before the knot is concealed inside the fastener. Remember to tie the knot *after* threading through the hole

Crimping beads are small beads of metal, used to secure gut or cable, which connect to a fastener loop by gripping tight. Start and finish the threaded necklace with a crimping bead (a). Connect the gut or cable with the fastener loop at each end and pass it through the crimping bead and the next couple of beads (b). Pull the ends of the gut to push the beads close up to the fastener and secure by squeezing the crimping bead with snipe-nosed pliers (c) pliers until it is flat and grips the cable and prevents it being able to slide out again. The cable end has to be cut very close or it will be scratchy. Small wire cutters or side cutters (they look like toe-nail clippers) are best for this.

6 GIMP, BULLION OR PURL

Using gimp, bullion or purl on a threaded necklace knotted onto a fastener is the simplest traditional way that I have developed for teaching to students. With practice it will be tidy, and is suitable for most precious gemstones or other rare and valuable beads. The advantage of this method is that there is only one knot with 'ends' in the whole necklace. Although I have seen variants of this knot in use, to my knowledge no other printed instructions for stringing include this one. Knotting between beads is a development from this basis (see pages 40-3).

Gimp, bullion, purl, French wire or necklet ends are alternative names for a fine silver, gold or plated tubular wire coil, used to protect thread which passes through fastener loops

Gimp, bullion (sometimes incorrectly called bouillon), purl, French wire or necklet ends are alternative names for small coiled 'springs' of very fine silver, or silver-gilt wire (also used sometimes as an ingredient of gold and silver embroidery). Made in several thicknesses and qualities, it can be cut with fine scissors to exact lengths as required and used to cover the exposed thread at each end where it goes through the fastener. It protects the thread while at the same time disguising it and makes a visually pleasing transition between beads and metal fastener. Gimp needs special handling, and unlike a spring, if pulled out, squashed or bent, it does not return to its former shape.

Lay out your beads in order. Using double thread with a wire needle and at least 30cm (12in) extra length, start by securing the doubled end of the thread with a slip knot, or any temporary knot. Then thread the first end bead, A. Carefully thread 6mm (¼in) of gimp over the thread, followed by the bolt-ring half of your fastener. Then without any knot go back through bead A in the reverse direction from before, followed by B, C, and the whole sequence of beads to X, Y, Z. Put the split ring half of the fastener and a second piece of gimp of the same length on to your thread. Now *do not cut the thread,* but untwist your wire needle and

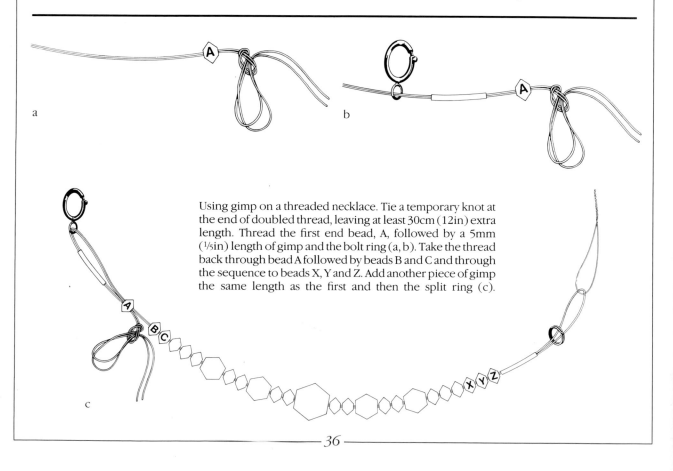

a

b

c

Using gimp on a threaded necklace. Tie a temporary knot at the end of doubled thread, leaving at least 30cm (12in) extra length. Thread the first end bead, A, followed by a 5mm (⅕in) length of gimp and the bolt ring (a, b). Take the thread back through bead A followed by beads B and C and through the sequence to beads X, Y and Z. Add another piece of gimp the same length as the first and then the split ring (c).

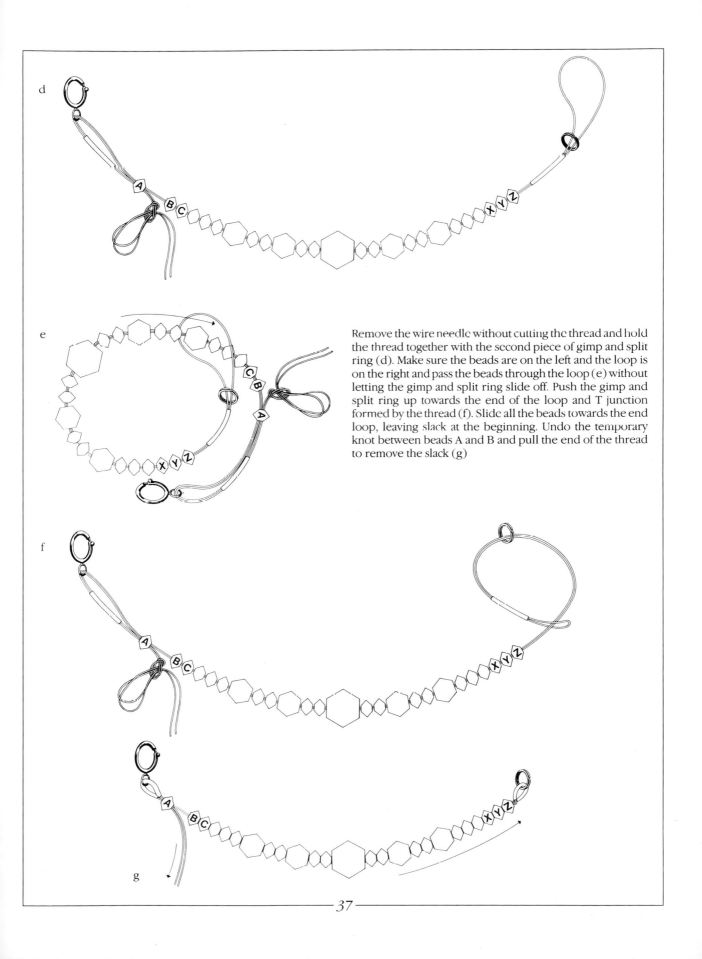

d

e

Remove the wire needle without cutting the thread and hold the thread together with the second piece of gimp and split ring (d). Make sure the beads are on the left and the loop is on the right and pass the beads through the loop (e) without letting the gimp and split ring slide off. Push the gimp and split ring up towards the end of the loop and T junction formed by the thread (f). Slide all the beads towards the end loop, leaving slack at the beginning. Undo the temporary knot between beads A and B and pull the end of the thread to remove the slack (g)

f

g

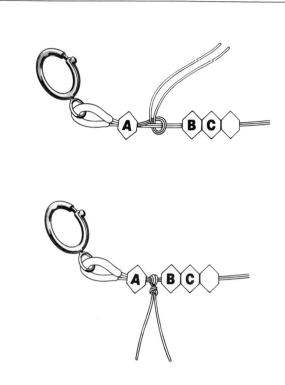

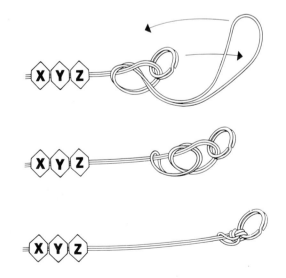

Tie a half-hitch knot with the doubled ends over the centre thread, and, taking each strand separately, pass them over and under the centre thread in opposite directions. Tie an overhand knot and tighten by pulling the two strands away from each other. The knot will now sit on the main thread

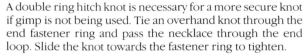

A double ring hitch knot is necessary for a more secure knot if gimp is not being used. Tie an overhand knot through the end fastener ring and pass the necklace through the end loop. Slide the knot towards the fastener ring to tighten.

take it right off, leaving the loop end of the thread intact. Securely grasp the thread where it emerges from bead Z, keeping the beads on the left, and the gimp, fastener ring and remaining loop of the doubled thread on the right. Adjust your hold to prevent gimp and fastener sliding around. Without letting go of the gimp and fastener and without letting them slide off the end, put the whole of the rest of the necklace *through* the loop. Relax your grasp at point G, and slide the gimp and fastener along to the end of the loop, towards the 'T' junction formed by the thread. The whole end loop and fastener is now able to slide up and tighten, like a noose, which will remain permanently held in place attached to the fastener without any ugly or lumpy knot. This knot is called a ring hitch. (When you have mastered the principle you may find your own way to arrive at the same knot.)

Now to finish, slide all the beads Z, Y, X, etc. back towards the end just completed so that all the slack will now be at the beginning, at beads A, B, C. Undo the temporary knot which is located between beads A and B. Pull out all the extra slack, carefully. Provided the beads, thread sizes and gimp have been well matched, this end will also begin to look right. Take these two tail strands of thread together. Tie a half-hitch with them around the centre thread – a firm pull will tighten up any remaining slack. Take each strand separately, one towards you, under the main thread and up the other side, and take the other strand in the opposite direction, away from you and down the other side. Tie an overhand knot with the two strands together and tighten it by pulling the strands smartly away from each other, so the knot sits right down next to the main thread. This is the only knot on the whole necklace, and should be almost invisible. Cut off close, and singe just enough to seal with a tiny blob. Although not necessary, you could also take the threads through another bead, B, and repeat the knot.

If you are using this method without gimp, the knot at bead Z by itself is less satisfactory as the loop tends to separate, unless you make an additional pass with the loop which forms a double ring hitch. It will also slide up and tighten like a noose, and holds the two strands closer together.

If strict symmetry is desired, then another knot to balance could be tied between the fastener and bead A, before tying your final knot. Instead of gimp, a 6mm (⅕in) length of embroidery beads could be used, threaded on the loop.

7 KNOTTING BETWEEN BEADS

This technique is a refinement of the previous one. Knots between beads fulfil several functions: they pro-

tect the necklace (if it breaks, no more than one bead would fall off), they protect the beads from grinding against each other, they economise by allowing fewer beads to cover the same length, they provide an additional visual element, adding an accent of harmonising or contrasting colour, and the whole necklace hangs more elegantly even if the stones are unevenly drilled. Some precious or highly ornate beads definitely look much better if slightly separated. Each knot will use up extra thread, so allow up to three times the calculated length of the finished necklace of *doubled* thread. Try to match up the sizes of holes in the beads you intend to use, employing the thickest double, or double-doubled thread that will fit through the smallest-holed of your beads. You can experiment later with patterns of larger- and smaller-holed beads together.

Start as method 6, with a temporary knot, bead A, gimp, fastener ring, back through A, then B, C, to X, Y, Z, taking care not to tangle the additional length. Then add the gimp and other fastener ring, and take off the wire needle without cutting the thread, leaving a loop, as before. Tie a ring hitch as described before, with the gimp and fastener held securely next to the end

Two views of a Victorian seed pearl necklace, in its own velvet-lined box, with close-up showing construction at the back of the centre unit

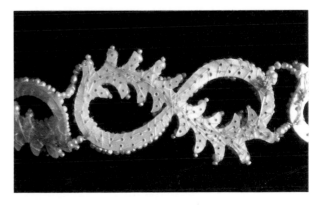

bead Z. You may find it helps to fix the ring with a nail or drawing pin or T pin onto your work surface or a piece of pinboard, but this is not essential. The first knot comes next to bead Z, before sliding up bead Y. Make a loose overhand knot in the two strands of thread, then tighten it up close, by one of these methods.

DARNING NEEDLE

Keep the work flat on the surface in front of you without any bits dangling that could pull unnecessarily. Hold (or pin) the fastener end, including bead Z, down, and press the fine point of a strong large darning needle or similar tool, through the loop of the overhand knot, against bead Z and onto the table surface, then you can pull the thread away from it to tighten up the knot around the point of the needle. This can be removed at the last minute and the knot can be 'firmed up' by pulling the two strands away from each other to tighten the very last bit. Glue should be completely unnecessary even if you are using silk. Repeat after sliding up each successive bead.

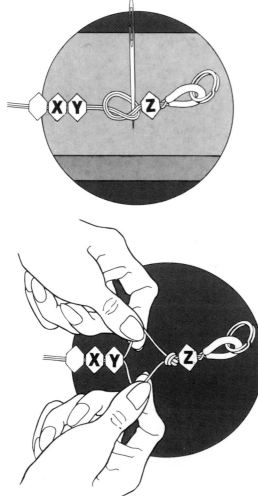

When tightening a knot between beads the fastener end with bead Z can be held or pinned down. Put a darning needle through the loop of the overhand knot, down onto the work surface. Press it against bead Z so that the thread may be pulled away and the knot tightened around the needle. Remove the needle and tighten the remaining slack by pulling the strands away from each other

WATCHMAKER'S TWEEZERS

These are a precision tool, milled to a very slender and exact long tapered point. They are expensive and should be reserved for fine work only.

Use the fine point of the tweezers through the loop of the knot as with the darning needle, but grip the double thread where it emerges from bead Z, allowing the loop of the knot to surround its point. Pull up the excess thread so the loop is forced to tighten around the tweezer point, next to bead Z. Slide the tweezers out at the last minute and hold them over the thread where it emerges from the knot and press the knot tight, firmly against the bead from the outside.

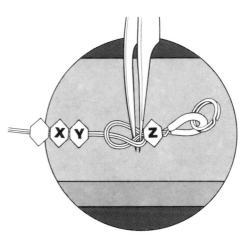

Instead of positioning a knot with a needle, watchmaker's tweezers may be used for the same purpose. Put the fine point of the tweezers through the loop of the knot and grip the thread emerging from bead Z with the tweezers. Pull the excess thread so the knot tightens around the tweezers. Remove the tweezers and use them to hold the thread emerging from the knot and then press the knot against bead Z

FINGERS

You may prefer not to use tools at all. In this case, hold the necklace in your hand, with your thumb-nail under the knot, below bead Z. Push the knot up with your nail and with practice your other fingers and other hand will get used to being able to pull down the extra thread away from the knot, while your thumb-nail keeps the knot pressed against bead Z. Again it can be additionally tightened by separating the strands and pulling away from each other, although this will not be necessary as you become more adept if you choose this method. With knotting, it is important to keep your overhand knots consistent and rhythmical, always right over left, or left over right, with equal tension. If you swap the ends from one hand to the other, or put it down and pick up later, remember to continue as you began, right over left or

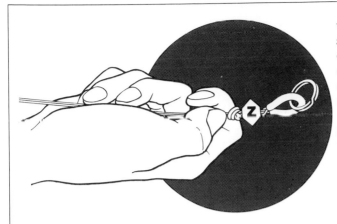

If you do not wish to use any tools, you can use your fingers to tighten a knot. Hold the necklace in one hand with your thumb-nail placed against the knot next to bead Z. Pull the excess thread away with your fingers and other hand while you *push* the knot tight with your thumb-nail. Slide the next bead along and continue

Finishing a knotted necklace. Slide bead B down towards the knot and bead C, and undo the temporary knot between beads A and B. Pull up any slack to secure the gimp and fastener next to A. Tie a half-hitch with the two strands around the centre thread, pull firm, and take each strand around opposite sides of the centre thread. Tie an overhand knot, tighten it down to the thread and cut any protruding thread, or singe the ends if you are using nylon thread.

An alternative method of hiding the ends is to pull both strands or one at a time through bead B with a wire needle. To avoid the ends working loose, put a drop of clear nail varnish or *soluble* adhesive on the thread just before you pull it inside the beads to anchor it in position

vice versa, and the knots will remain a consistent shape. It is slightly better to over-tighten as the effect of any pulling tends to compact the knots, pulling out extra lengths of thread at each side of the knots. Also, there are some threads that do stretch. Pass the beads along one at a time, knotting after each one.

Stop knotting next to bead C

Push down bead B, undo the temporary knot and pull up all the extra slack to secure the gimp and fastener next to A. As with method 6, take the two tail strands and make a half-hitch around the centre strands, pull firm, separate, and have them meet around the other side, then with both strands together, make an overhand knot, tighten it down and cut off the extra protruding tails. If nylon thread is used, singe the whiskers into a fine tiny blob.

You can otherwise make the ends disappear by pulling both strands together, or one at a time, down through bead B by using the wire needle, loop end first like a needle threader, up through bead B and then with one or both strands threaded through its loop, it can be pulled back down through bead B. If you think the ends may work loose, put a tiny drop of clear nail varnish, gum, or other *soluble* adhesive onto the thread just before you pull it through, to anchor it into position.

Do not use superglue or Araldite on thread to go inside a bead as it is guaranteed to make the bead completely unusable, entailing a complete redrilling job.

Alternative knots between beads A and B

If you wish to try to keep the last knot less bulky, try either of the following techniques. Their only drawbacks are that the knots are much more difficult to tighten effectively.

REEF KNOT AROUND THE CENTRE THREAD

With the two tails separated, tie the first half of a reef knot, then take each tail around the centre thread and finish the reef knot. Cut the tails off and apply a tiny dot of glue to secure. Without glue it would work loose and undo.

'MATTHEW WALKER' KNOT WITH 2 STRANDS

Follow the illustration to tie the knot. Cut the ends off close – a tiny dot of glue will be needed to prevent unravelling.

'Streamlining' the ends

Sometimes on repair jobs with fine beads you may need to use only one double thickness to go through gimp and fastener, even though the rest of the actual

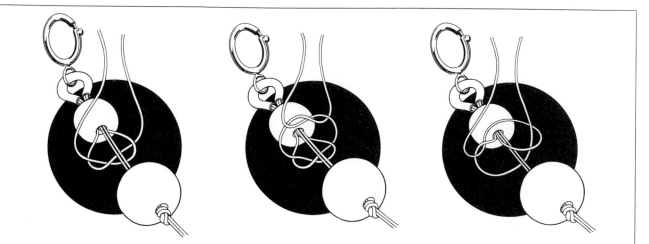

(left and *centre)* Tying a reef knot around the centre thread between two beads. Tie the first half of a reef knot under the main thread (a), take the strands around the thread and finish the knot (b)

(right) Matthew Walker knot around the centre thread, a method using two strands

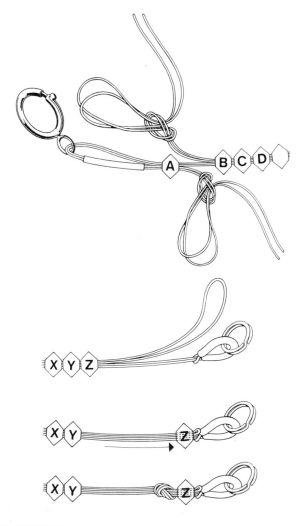

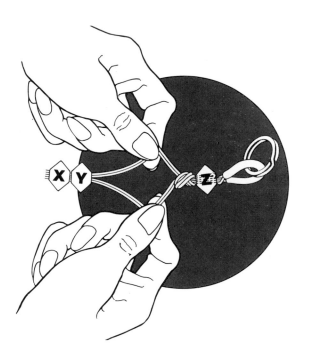

Often beads will take two double thicknesses of thread, whereas the gimp and fastener will only take one. Add a second thread in the usual way after attaching gimp and fastener, so a double thickness goes through beads B, C, D up to the last few, X, Y and Z. Take off one double thickness of thread from the needle and attach gimp and fastener with the ring hitch knot. You will now have one extra loop (b). Slide bead Z towards the gimp loop, keeping the second loop protruding (c). Tie an overhand knot between beads Z and Y as usual (d). As you tighten it the protruding loop should disappear inside bead Z (e)

beads would take two double thicknesses and the knots would look better bigger. Naturally, the thread next to the fastener has to endure more wear than anywhere else, but it is sometimes practical and possible to attach fasteners with the one double thickness, immediately adding another double thread of the same length to work the sequence of beads with their knots.

After threading on the end beads X, Y, Z, take one double thread off the needle. Keep it out of the way to avoid it tangling, and proceed to attach gimp and fastener with the self-tightening ring hitch knot as normal. Now, slide bead Z next to the gimp loop, keeping the second loop just protruding. Make your first overhand knot between Z and Y as usual. As you tighten it the protruding loop should just disappear inside bead Z, and is now sufficiently attached to allow you to do the rest as normal.

When you get back to the first beads, knot as usual between C and B, then pull up the slack between B and A to tighten the gimp and fastener as before, but knot the four strands together with one of the finishing knots described in this chapter.

MULTISTRAND AND PENDANT THREADING
and other Useful Techniques

MULTISTRAND CONSTRUCTION

Bracelets and wide chokers that sit like a band around the throat are best made with broad fasteners that have a row of holes or loops (usually three, five, or seven) to attach to the strands. A normal bracelet is at least 18cm (7in) long, but a true close-fitting choker would have to be individually fitted, as neck sizes vary upwards from 37cm (14½in). On a proper 'dog collar' choker, the strands are parallel and scarcely need any variation in length.

To keep the strands evenly spaced and together like a strip, 'spacers' can be used. These are usually made of a pierced metal strip, or other material such as plastic, bone, or leather, or the same stone as the beads.

With inexpensive beads you can attach the fastener loops with callottes or bead tips. It is usually easier to thread up completely and attach one strand at a time. Where a multistrand necklace has a top and bottom edge, remember to arrange the fastener correctly for a right-handed person unless otherwise instructed. This means when the necklace is put on, the right hand can manipulate while the left hand holds.

If you use precious beads (chokers are so often made with pearls), you will want to knot properly. Either forget about the ring hitch knot and work both ends of each strand like the A, B, C ending described on page 41, with tails of loose thread, adding a needle to attach and return through the end beads where necessary (you will have to do it this way if using spacer bars). Alternatively, complete each row without attaching to the clasp, and join the ends in turn to the *same* half of the clasp with the ring hitch knot. Undo the temporary knot and add a needle to each strand in turn to attach at the other end with gimp and clasp, then go back through bead A of each string and make a secure knot.

It is easier to avoid getting in a tangle while working if you put a small clear plastic bag over all the loose strands not in use to hold their tails together, out of the way. Partly close the bag if necessary with an elastic band.

Practise these techniques on a bracelet.

If a wide enough clasp is not available there exist metal end spacers which have a row of holes on one edge and a single hole on the other side which connects directly to a single loop fastener or to a threaded length of beads or chain. These are more commonly used for multistrand necklaces that are longer and have strands of graduated lengths. It is almost impossible to establish rules about lengths, because of the varied sizes of the beads themselves, but it may help to create multistrand designs using an old-fashioned tailor's or dressmaker's dummy, so that strands can be tried out and matched up. When worn, the aim is to avoid the beads in the centre of each strand touching, yet not to have them too far apart. When using spacer bars on these necklaces, remember to allow them to radiate from a central point (towards the back of the neck).

With multistrand chokers and bracelets a multistrand snap fastener can be used to attach the strands. Spacers keep the strands together and evenly spaced

Attaching a multistrand fastener using the ring hitch knot method. For five strands: start each row of beads with a temporary knot, then the sequence of beads A–Z, finish with gimp. Remove the needle without cutting the thread and attach each of the five strands with the ring hitch knot to one of the rings on the first half of the clasp, by passing the threaded beads through the loop, as before. Then, for each strand in turn, undo the temporary knot at the beginning of the row, attach a needle and thread through gimp and the appropriate ring on the second half of the fastener, and take the thread back through bead A, making a firm knot as before to finish

Metal end spacers have a row of loops on one edge and a single loop on the other which attaches to a fastener or threaded length of beads or chain. This choker has a hook fastening

Twisting

Many multistrand necklaces are in fact a bunch of at least three equal strands, twisted to appear like a loose rope. These can be made to hold a permanent twist as follows. At the fastener, all the strands need to come together, in an overhand knot. Provided this knot is fairly small, one callotte will hold all the strands on the fastener loop, otherwise they should be securely knotted onto a wire eyepin, in turn concealed underneath a bell cap or bead cup.

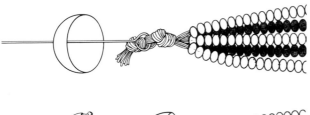

A twisted multistrand necklace can be fastened with a callotte and bolt ring or, if the knot is too big, with a bell cap. Secure the strands with a firm overhand knot, and make a second one over an eyepin. Take the eyepin through the bell cap and attach a bolt ring

To create the twist, with one end already attached and secured down to a hook or nail, and the other bunch of ends loose, take one row at a time and twist anticlockwise, *at least* fifteen complete twists for a choker length. Pin it down or grip it in such a way that it cannot untwist while you do the same with the other strands. Now, with care, gather all the strands together without losing their individual twists and hold them tight. Unhook the other end and let it hang downwards. The whole rope of beads should now magically twist up around itself. Knot the remaining gathered ends together with an overhand knot, making sure that no bare thread is left, and the twist is evenly distributed. The 'rope' should keep its twist. Attach a bolt ring or flat ornamental clasp, not a swivelling barrel or screw fastener.

Removing beads

If you discover a bead too many, and it is inconvenient to unthread the whole operation, you can remove an inexpensive bead of glass or some other material if necessary by breaking it. To avoid cutting the thread at the same time, use snipe-nosed pliers and, gripping *parallel* to the thread, not across it, squeeze smartly like a nutcracker.

To remove an unwanted small glass bead, you can break it with snipe-nosed pliers. Always grip *parallel* to the thread, not across it

Changing thread

To change the thread you have just threaded for an entire new or longer length without unthreading the sequence of beads, or for clean thread, remove the needle without cutting the loop of the thread, loop the new thread through the old thread, knot with a temporary knot at the further end or a weaver's knot (see diagram) near the loop, and slide all the beads across to the new thread. By using this technique you can also simply extend your existing thread if you want room to thread more beads. Just move the knotted ends of the old or new thread close to the join, but not right on top of it. The knot at the end of the thread should be a reef knot or weaver's knot, as they have less volume and may slide inside a bead to conceal the join.

Knotting between beads with fat holes

It is generally better to choose a 'thread' of many strands of thinner thread rather than a fat cord. This allows you scope for blending colours, and, when knotted, the knot will compact neatly into a little round cushion. Fat cord tends to make a more lopsided knot.

Knotting hints

Remember that an overhand knot is a lump about three times the thickness of the thread with which it is tied. A so-called double overhand knot (one more overhand knot tied on top of the first) is very unreliable. When pulled a few times it may slip off and make another ordinary knot next to, not on top of, the original one. A double knot (blood knot) and a figure of eight knot may appear to have extra volume but they tend to pull out to a long sort of lump that is still only about as thick as an overhand knot, but makes the strung necklace look loose, and is hard to control as it is tightened.

Ideas for fasteners

If you find the addition of a manufactured metal clasp looks out of keeping with the rest of the necklace, you could try variations on some of these ideas.

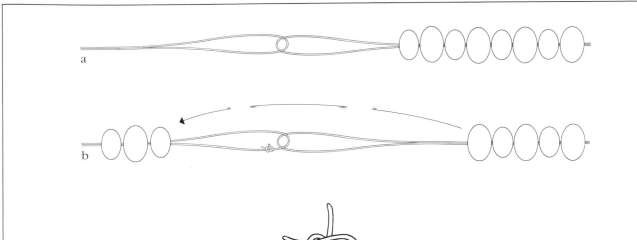

a

b

c

Changing thread. Remove the needle without cutting the loops of the old thread and loop the new thread through the old (a). Tie a temporary knot at the end of the new thread. Tie the ends of the new thread with a weaver's knot (c) near the join with the old and slide the beads across to the new thread (b)

BUTTON AND BUTTONHOLE
A buttonhole loop can be constructed at one end of the necklace using the cord on which the beads are threaded as the core, around which either whipping, buttonhole stitch, a macramé stitch or a length of embroidery beads can be added to make a solid buttonhole loop as illustrated. The button itself can be a button, a bead, a beaded bead or a knot.

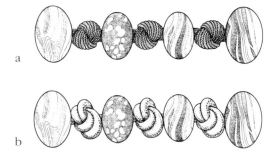

a

b

Use many strands of thinner thread when knotting between beads with large holes, to give more flexibility with colours and a more compact, neat knot (a). Thicker cord will give a less attractive, lopsided knot (b)

S SHAPE
You can use an S shape of copper, brass, or silver wire, hammered hard to keep its shape, with a ring or another S into which it will slot. This looks more in keeping with ancient or primitive beads than a mass-produced shiny new clasp.

Copper, brass or silver wire can be hammered to give an S shape clasp which attaches to a ring or another S

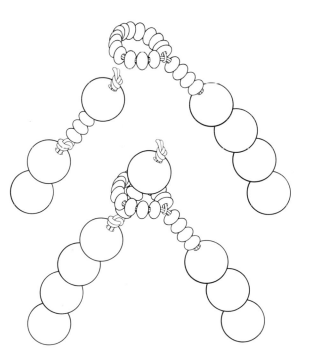

Button and buttonhole fastening. The button can be a bead and the buttonhole a loop of embroidery beads to fit neatly over the 'button'

The sliding bead can be a matching bead or contrast with those in the necklace. Allow enough extra thread for the necklace when extended to go over the head. Draw up the bead to tighten to the desired length

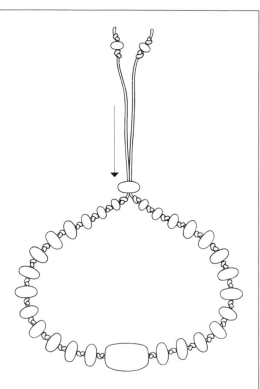

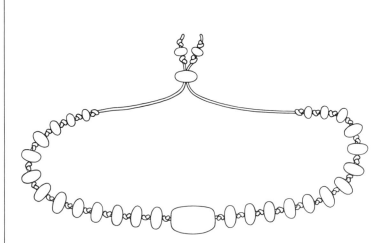

SLIDING KNOT
This is used in leather thong especially for bracelets or chokers (shown on page 29).

SLIDING BEAD
Many of the more precious bead necklaces from India are, or used to be, threaded with long braided cords of silk and gold thread, with both ends passing through a snug-fitting bead-shaped Turk's head knot, or a matching bead which slides up and down. When extended, the necklace goes over the head, then the bead is drawn up to tighten, and two cords dangle decoratively down at the back, sometimes with coloured silk tassels below a 'stop bead', or knot, on each. It has the advantage of offering a choice of lengths without a commitment to being a long or a short necklace, although it is always a closed loop.

Braided ends
A string of beads can also have attractive thick braided ends or cords that will tie at any length you choose. Even if the cord or braid used for going through the beads has to be quite thin, extra strands can be added at the end of the sequence of beads so that it appears to be that thick all the way through.

For good, substantial braided ends, make them at least 15cm (6in), plus an extra 15cm (6in) for knot and tassel at each end (60cm [24in] longer than total length of bead sequence). To join two or more extra strands

to the two already there, separate the two strands where they come out of the end bead, then prepare the strands to be added – they should be two double lengths, 60cm (24in) each, if you want a total of six. Lay them mid-point across and between the two original strands, which are then brought together to make the first half of a reef knot. Pulled tight, this is quite sufficient to begin a nice firm braid. If you have six strands you could make a normal flat plait with three doubles, divide them into three pairs and start plaiting firmly, pulling the knot close as you start. With four strands in total, a good round braid can be made (like one of the 'scooby doo' stitches), as illustrated. Make a firm knot at the end.

TWISTED CORDS
This works better with a quantity of fine threads together. Allow plenty of extra length. Knot the threads after the end bead. Divide the threads into two or three equal bunches, and twist each bunch clockwise separately. It is easier to do this with the opposite end attached to something, a hook or nail in the table or doorpost, for instance. Hold down one section while twisting the other. Count your twists to make sure the other bunches are even. Without letting them unravel, knot the ends of the twisted bunches together, then unhook the opposite end to let it twist on itself. Mixed colours can be used to great effect, harmonising with the beads in the necklace.

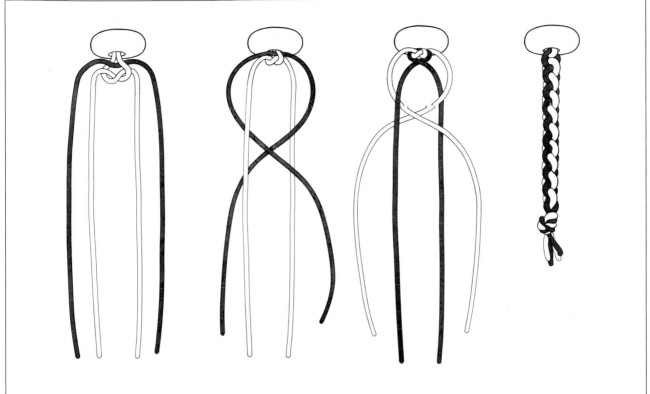

Adding extra strands for a braided cord end. Thread the beads on double thread, allowing a generous extra length at each end, cut two or more additional threads (double the required length) at each end and position them centrally between the two strands where they emerge from the bead at one end. Bring the two strands together and tie the first half of a reef knot over the added strands to keep them in place. Now plait or braid the bunched ends ending with a firm overhand knot, and trim the ends to form a tassel. Repeat at the other end

Twisted cords are best worked with a number of strands together – allow plenty of extra length. Tie a knot after the end bead and divide the threads into two or three equal bunches. Twist each bunch separately in a clockwise direction, having held the necklace end of the bunch down to prevent the rest of the thread from twisting. Ensure the twists are the same number in each bunch, and knot the ends together. Then release the other end to let the cord twist on itself

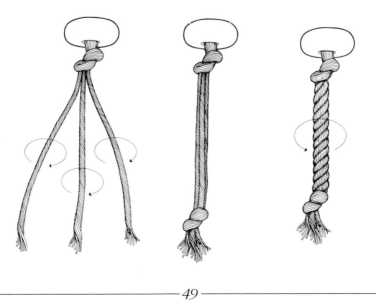

MACRAMÉ

All sorts of personal ornaments can be made using the techniques of macramé, which can be quite charming or impressive when well done. Beads are often incorporated in the patterns to great effect. There are a lot of excellent specialist books on the subject, and in this context I shall only mention the macramé techniques that contribute to bead necklace construction.

As well as the braids already described, macramé techniques could be used at each end, adding as before, for the braids, one extra long doubled cord which would allow a good solid layer of 'flat knots' or a spiral of 'half-knots' around the original doubled 'leader' or core thread where it emerges from the beads at each end. The ends can be concealed inside the end bead. Macramé can also be used as a neat alternative to whipping on buttonholes or to wrap one or more cords between the end of the bead sequence and the fastener loop, or used to gather several strands. It looks well done with a third cord or string for a necklace of beads of substantial size with large holes and knots between. When planning this sort of necklace, allow a lot of extra length since at the finish, for example of 5cm (2in) of macramé plait, you need extra tails of at least 20cm (8in). Once again the advantage is that next to the fastener there is no knot

with messy ends, and the thread is finished off at a point where it is much more visually acceptable to have a slightly irregular lump.

PENDANTS

A pendant differs from a bead because it has its hole at one end ('the top') or it has a loop, usually of wire. A large or long bead can become a pendant if it is hung vertically with a knot or tassel, or on a wire with a loop. Earrings are often made of beads in this way. Most usually a pendant is drop-shaped and often flat. Carved and shaped stone pendants very often have a front-to-back hole. If threaded exactly as they are between beads, they will hang sideways. Some have a small wire loop bent in a triangular shape or 'bail', so that they would lie flat if threaded or hung on a chain. To avoid using a visible metal component, a pendant can be made to hang flat on thread. It will not be possible to attach a fastener to a pendant necklace with the usual ring hitch, but the necklace can be designed with knots as usual.

After threading the whole sequence, including the pendant in the centre, put another slip knot at the needle and loop end to stop any beads sliding off. Hold up the two ends together and let the pendant

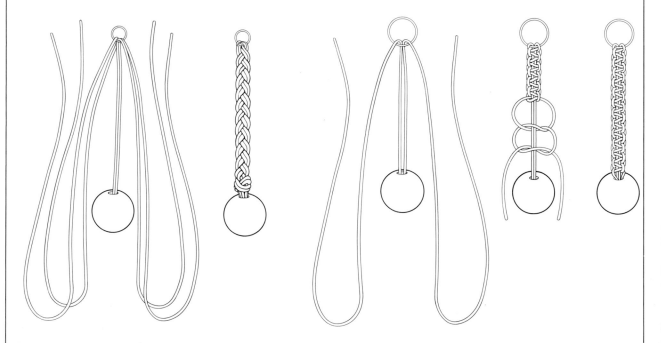

Plaited ends avoid the use of a bulky knot to attach to a fastener. Allow plenty of extra doubled thread which should go through the end ring. Start plaiting from the ring downwards towards the beads and finish with an overhand knot

For macramé ends, allow an extra long length of doubled cord, at least four times the desired length, and work your design around the doubled 'leader' or thread emerging from the end bead. The ends can be concealed inside the end bead

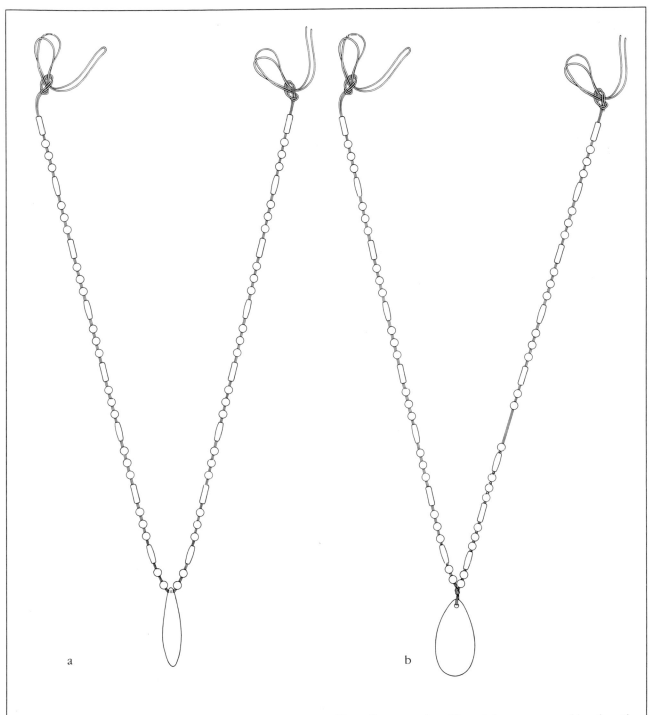

a

b

Threading a pendant. Thread the sequence of beads with the pendant in the middle. Tie temporary knots at the ends to prevent any beads from sliding off. The pendant will, at this stage, be hanging sideways (a). Taking hold of the pendant, make enough slack in the thread to tie an overhand knot immediately above it, and push it down against the pendant. Slide the beads down towards the pendant, knotting between each one (b). At the fastener end you will have to double back through the beads at both ends when attaching the fastener

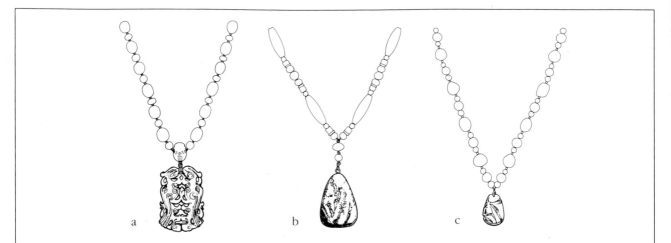

a   b   c

Alternative methods of attaching a pendant to a necklace: (a) a bead can be drilled with a T shaped hole to hold the thread and the hanging pendant; (b) the pendant can hang from a couple of beads separated by overhand knots; and (c) a threaded loop of tiny embroidery beads can hold the pendant

(below) To attach a fastener with thong, taper the end of the thong to a long, pointed wedge shape. Pass it through the end bead and the fastener ring, fold it over and squeeze it through the end bead again with the help of some glue, then press it down tight so it rests against bead Y and bring the end bead as far down to meet it as possible

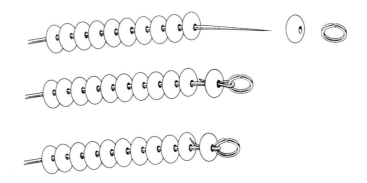

slide towards the centre of the thread. Keeping the beads out of the way for the moment take hold of the pendant and tie an overhand knot in the two strands together. Push it down to tighten against the pendant. Now, first with one strand, then the other, slide the beads down one at a time towards the pendant, knotting as usual. At the fastener end, you will need to 'double back' with both lots of ends when attaching the fastener, or devise another kind of join such as cords, or a knot and tassel. This pendant type of necklace needs to be at least 65cm (26in) to have the right 'important' look to it, and to dangle properly, like a medallion.

When designing a necklace using a series of smaller pendants of this sort, remember that they will hang downwards, not outwards. Small side pendants may flop forward to show their backs.

Sometimes with very large holed beads, thong is much more appropriate than thread or braid because of the solid way it articulates, but a good fastener, not a cheap one, is desired. It can be attached with the help of a glue such as Uhu: using a craft knife, taper off the end of the thong to a long narrow flat wedge shape. Put it through the last bead and the fastener loop, fold over and squeeze it back through the last bead with a touch of the glue, then press down tight to secure it. Do the same at the other end, tightening it by pulling the tip of the tapered end.

5
BEADS WITH WIRE
Earrings, Necklaces, Brooches, Cufflinks

This is an area which requires an extension to the range of tools and techniques. See illustration on page 25.

Pliers: round-nosed pliers for forming and opening and closing wire links and jump rings.

Snipe-nosed pliers have a fine tapering rounded end with smooth flat jaws inside (looking like Concorde), useful for delicately gripping and manipulating in small areas.

Flat-nosed pliers are the same as snipe-nosed, but without the tapering point.

Chainlink or rosary pliers combine round-nosed pliers with wire cutters.

Wire cutters have cutting jaws rather like toe-nail cutters. If sufficiently fine, they will reach into corners to cut close.

EARRINGS

In recent years, small fortunes have been made (and lost) and countless summer holidays abroad have been financed by the manufacture and sale of bead earrings by the low-technology, one-person peripatetic production-line business. All that is needed is a bagful of beads in fashion colours, plenty of eyepins or a roll of wire, a quantity of hooks (preferably 'kidney wires'), and a pair of round-nosed pliers. Simple basic bead earrings are very easy to make up. The loop at the top of the eyepin is formed with round-nosed pliers, and is then bent back towards the centre at its neck. When attached to any earring clasp, make sure the loops are bent completely closed so as not to come apart. Headpins are very similar to eyepins, having a knob instead of a loop at the bottom end, which does not show. They are generally available in softer wire than eyepins. A large-holed bead is kept in place by a small bead beneath it. Attach a pendant with a wire triangle or 'bail'. The basic unit of a bead or beads on wire with a loop at each end is also the component link of a necklace chain and also known as the S link. Necklaces made in this way are of course economical on beads although they are all too often badly made and can look cheap. Sometimes the

wire ends of the S links protrude and catch on clothing, or, when pulled, the whole chain starts to bend open and the links disconnect. The hooked links with beads on cannot be soldered or the beads would be damaged.

There are some beautiful necklaces made this way with gold wire and small gemstones. Each link has a loop which is finished off with an extra twist around the stem, making it look and feel solid. Make sure the pieces you wish to link are already looped on before closing the link. When buying ready-made chain, choose the kind with links that are soldered shut. You will have to cut a link here and there when separating it into short lengths, but the difference is remarkable. A small pull on a cheap chain is quite enough to open links along its entire length. Remember, a chain is only as strong as its weakest link.

The normal fastening for a chain is a bolt ring and a jump ring. If the bolt ring has a ring with an opening, it can simply be bent open in a twisting, sideways

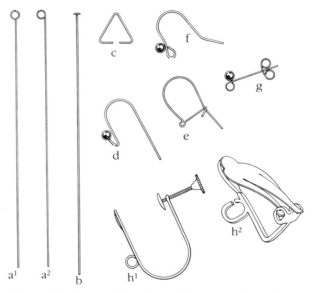
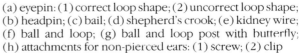

(a) eyepin: (1) correct loop shape; (2) uncorrect loop shape; (b) headpin; (c) bail; (d) shepherd's crook; (e) kidney wire; (f) ball and loop; (g) ball and loop post with butterfly; (h) attachments for non-pierced ears: (1) screw; (2) clip

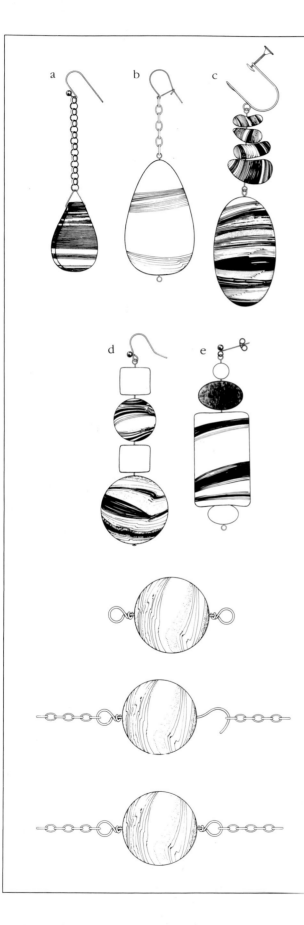

motion (as described in Chapter 3), linked through the end of the chain and pressed back together. Otherwise, if the ring is soldered shut, use an appropriate jump ring to make the link which connects the two.

Beads on wire links can also make pendants for necklaces, either large central pendants or lavish quantities of beads, like blossom or fruit, to dangle all along a threaded or chain necklace, or brooch. For earrings and this type of necklace, some glass drops are formed directly onto wire, which can then be bent into a loop, often in the shapes of flowers, petals, fruit and foliage or plain drops. Some of the most perennially popular and charming glass-bead choker necklaces from Venice include clusters of these components as leaves, fruits, blossoms and even birds, insects or fish. Surprisingly they need not be prickly, as the bunches all point away from the skin when worn.

(*above* and *right*)
Beads on wire, flowers and doll's-house chair
Maasai collars of beads on wire, with earrings from Kenya

(*above left*) Basic earring construction variations: (a) drop pendant with wire bail; (b) drop-shaped bead on eyepin; (c) beads on eyepin with screw attachment; (d) beads on head-pin with ball and loop attachment; (e) beads strung with eyepin attached to ball and loop post

(*left*) The two wire loops either side of the bead can be opened to connect to a chain, and are known as the S link. Care must be taken that the holes are closed completely tight and that they do not catch on clothing

BROOCHES

Some accessories enjoying a revival are beaded brooches, made with beads stitched with fine wire onto a perforated round or oval template which then clips onto a matching brooch back. They used to be popular in the sixties, along with large blossom-cluster earclips and hats covered with petals or dangly sequins (see Project 4).

To attach beads, decide your intended pattern, and use thin soft wire, such as brass picture wire or fuse wire. The pattern illustrated has three concentric areas. The outside ring of petal-shaped beads is threaded up, the ends securely twisted together and cut. Do the same with the middle ring of beads. With a separate piece of wire, link the centre beads directly onto the base, then use one strand of that wire to come up from behind, go round the wire of the middle ring and back, to hold it in at least four strategic places. Do the same with the outer ring of petals. All odd ends of wire at the back can be twisted together and cut, and they need not look neat as they will not show. The template can now be easily clamped onto the brooch back by bending the lugs around it.

The method is the same for cluster earrings, and can be used on the fasteners of some multistrand necklaces specially made to match, with perforated bases.

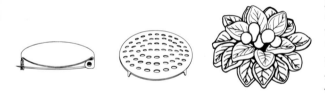

A beaded brooch is made with beads stitched with fine wire to a perforated template which clips to a matching back. Using brass picture or fuse wire, thread the outside ring of petal-shaped beads, twist the ends together and cut the wire. Do the same with the middle ring of beads independently. Taking another long piece of wire, thread the centre beads directly to the template, then come up from behind and through the wire of the middle ring and back with the extra length. Do this in at least four strategic places to hold it in position. Do the same with the outer ring of petals. Twist together any wire ends at the back and cut them, then attach the template to the back of the brooch by bending the lugs around it

CUFFLINKS

These can be made with figure of eight links, or a small length of chain between a pair of buttons with shanks, or flat beads. They need to be robust, and smooth enough not to damage the fabric of the shirt.

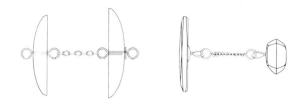

Cufflinks must be strong but at the same time smooth enough not to damage the shirt. They can be made with (a) disc beads separated by a small length of chain or (b) buttons with shanks held together with wire links

ORNAMENTS

All sorts of ornaments and items are made using beads on wire, which are summarised briefly here (see Bibliography for sources of more specialised information).

Lace bobbin spangles

Some of the traditional English lacemaking techniques use fine bobbins decoratively weighted and individualised by their 'spangles'. These are wire loops with usually seven or nine glass beads, one large, normally round, 'bottom bead', and then pairs of smaller beads often dice shaped ('square cut'), faceted or decorated. Information is difficult to obtain about their makers, origins and dates, but all these glass beads are quite distinctive with squiggle decoration, dots or eyes, with some of them having traditional names such as 'Kitty Fisher's eyes' or 'pompadours'. They may have been made from recycled bottle glass by itinerant craftsmen who peddled their wares at regular annual markets and fairs. Old Venetian beads from necklaces were also used. Favourite colours were white, clear, light blue, transparent green, transparent rose pink and transparent amber. They appear on the highly prized commemorative bobbins from the eighteenth century onwards.

Small beads used on wire are endlessly useful to anyone with a bit of fantasy. Entire Victorian flower arrangements, either multicoloured or in delicate frosty white alone, complete with butterflies, were treasured under glass domes, and doll's house furniture, Christmas tree decorations, tiny wire baskets, little people, encrusted mirror or picture frames, and, of course, not forgetting the beaded commemorative pincushion have all been made with beads.

Plain hatpins can be ornamented with amazing large beads held in place with a little glue. They are easier to use if the head of the pin is not too heavy.

The Maasai of Kenya use European rocaille beads

on iron or copper wire to create large, colourful, stiff collars of many rows of beads held parallel with wire or leather spacers, and also fanciful earrings and hair decorations which are interspersed with cowrie shells, buttons or triangular tin pendants.

In Angela Fisher's book *Africa Adorned,* there are many tribal garments and ornaments of beads on wire. Some of the most extraordinary are the 'corsets' of the Dinka, which are stiff garments made entirely of beads on wire, and worn by men. In theatre costume and for weddings and grand occasions, wreaths, tiaras and crowns can incorporate beads and wire to splendid effect, but generally, big wire structures are not very durable and therefore these items are for rare and one-off ceremonial or extravagant occasions only.

The *Young Ladies Journal* of 1 October 1866, has a pattern and instructions for an oval photograph frame cut out of white cardboard with a wreath of wire loops with 'glass and chalk beads' (clear and opaque glass) to be stitched onto the cardboard in overlapping layers.

Tiny glass embroidery beads were already being used on iron wire in England in the seventeenth century to build up baskets and ornate floral panels, in a style resembling Stuart 'stump work' embroidery.

Finger rings of beads and wire

You may come across a specially appealing bead, perhaps with a flat back that suggests a ring. If the bead has a reasonably sized hole, it will be fairly simple to pass a wire through it securely. Variations include two wires twisted together, through the hole, and coiled decoratively either side of the bead, or once through the bead, around the sides of the bead and wrapped around the further side.

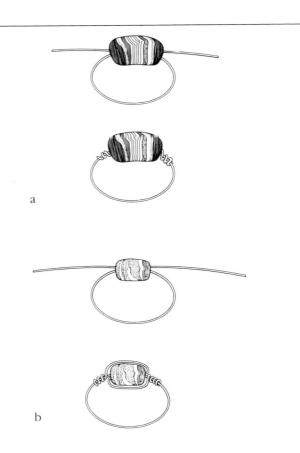

a

b

Variations in finger rings of beads and wire. Thread the wire through the bead, leaving the ends protruding. Coil these decoratively around the wire at the sides of the bead (a). Alternatively take one piece of wire as it protrudes from the bead over the top of the bead and then coil it round the side, and take the other end underneath the bead before coiling

6
REAL BEADWORK

On several occasions when I have given a talk to craft groups on the subject of beads, many people have come prepared to hear a talk on beadwork, which is generally understood to include beadweaving, bead lace and bead embroidery, the assumption being that beads by themselves are not sufficiently interesting. By now it will be clear that this is not the case!

However, beadwork is an interesting and extensive craft both to the collector and the practitioner, and ranges from primitive to highly sophisticated results, all demanding a high level of patience, attention and time in relation to a fairly simple skill. The techniques have been thoroughly covered in several good handicraft books (see Bibliography), so this chapter will be a basic summary of the various methods using embroidery beads and thread to create, or decorate, a fabric with beadwork patterns as an integral part of the structure.

Working with rocailles, or bugles, and thread, whether stitching onto fabric or not, requires a proper beading needle (see Chapter 2). When working a beadwork design with particular coloured beads, put out a small quantity of each different colour separately in small dishes. For a design requiring counted amounts of beads for each stitch, you will find that with practice, you will be able to pick up the right number of beads on the needle by plunging it into the dish. Although some of the rocaille beads are very small they have fairly generous and regular holes relative to their size (miniature doughnut shape), and can usually be threaded through more than once with a beading needle and fine thread (thread size 60).

BEADED FRINGES AND TASSELS

These may be parts of a necklace design or units in their own right, for earrings or brooches, etc. Fringes and tassels are composed of a row or bunch of 'ends', usually made with a threading structure that doubles back on itself, making the next end in the same way. Beaded tassels and loops can make exotic combinations with beads or they can be decorative in their own right, on earrings, for example, where their dangling and sparkling movement is particularly attractive.

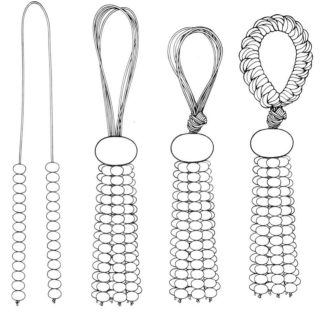

Beaded tassels can be threaded and pulled through a large-holed bead before knotting above the bead. The loop of strands can then be tidied up by using thicker thread and buttonhole stitch

To make tassels it is sufficient to thread up many short rows of beads, putting a good stout overhand knot at the bottom end of each strand, then gather the other ends together and knot securely. If using nylon thread, the whiskers of each end knot may be singed into a small neat blob to seal. The knot at the top can be hidden under a bell cap or all the threads can be pulled through one large-holed bead before being knotted.

Beaded fringes are a wonderful ornamental extra embellishment on short chokers, earrings, hairclips, lampshades, etc. A velvet ribbon decorated with a bead fringe becomes a sophisticated choker.

From top: beadwork choker by author, on wide multi-strand clasp. Macramé and beads bracelet. Four beadwoven chokers by Jo Pound and Marie Needham. Butterfly and crocodile of beads on wire. Brooch of beaded construction by Joyce J. Scott, USA

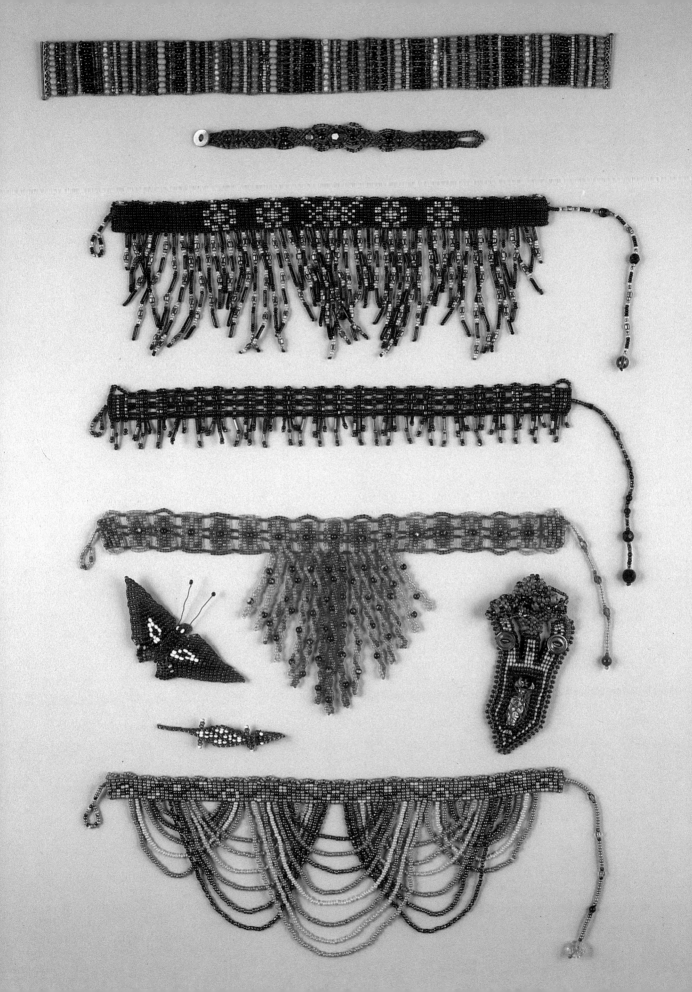

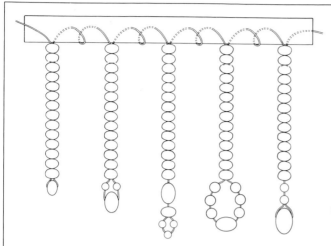

For beaded fringes always take the needle and thread down through the beads, through the end bead and up through the beads again, making a secure stitch in the material from which the fringe hangs before continuing along the length of beads. Choose what you like for your fringe ending.

The principle is the same as that for tassels, but the whole fringe would be much weaker if each strand finished with a cut end, so take the needle down through the beads, through the end bead and then back up through the others again, followed by a secure stitch or two into the support material it hangs from, and then down the next row of beads. (For a lampshade fringe, the strands generally hang from a cotton tape, which can be stitched onto the bottom edge of a shade or frame.)

Beadweaving chokers can have fringes worked as you go along, with the weft thread, or they can be stitched on later, which is easier to control and looks equally intentional. Some pieces of Zulu or Ndebele beadwork such as belts or necklaces have copious and dramatic fringes, which would naturally complement the movements of dance rhythms.

Basic bead lace patterns

These rely on variations of a kind of honeycomb-net construction pattern. Start with the simplest stitches. Following these basic patterns you can construct a parallel-edged strip of 18cm (7in) for a bracelet or 40cm (16in) for an attractive choker. For the fastening, the strip can either be stitched onto a 2- or 3-strand fastener, or the thread ends worked together and knotted onto a single loop fastener such as a bolt ring and split ring, or to make the length adjustable, stitch the ends of the strip onto ribbon or cord, which can be tied, or strips of Velcro. The 'Zulu beadwork' illustrated in colour uses the same honeycomb construction to make complex curved collar-shaped necklaces.

TWO THREADS (needle weaving)
A wider strip is easy to construct adding another thread and beads row, see illustration.

ONE THREAD
These patterns are easier to learn if the joining beads are a separate colour.
Thread 1 red bead A, 2 white, 1 red B, 5 white, 1 red C, 2 white, then back through red bead A, 5 white, 1 red D, 2 white, back through red bead C, 5 white, 1 red E, 2 white, etc.
This can be embellished with extra picot loops:
thread 1 red bead A, 2 white, 1 red B, 2 white, 1 red bead C, 3 white, back through bead C, then as follows:
2 white, red bead D, 2 white, back through bead A
2 white, red bead E, 3 white, back through bead E
2 white, red bead F, 2 white, back through bead D
2 white, red bead G, 3 white, back through bead G
2 white, red bead H, 2 white, back through bead F
2 white, red bead, I, 3 white, back through bead I
2 white, red bead J, 2 white, back through bead H, etc.

SINGLE DAISY
String with a single daisy every now and then (ten petals) green, white and yellow embroidery beads.
Thread 7 green, 6 white, 1 yellow, back in the opposite direction through 1st white; thread 4 whites, back through 6th white, 7 more green, etc.

CHAIN OF CONTINUOUS DAISIES, TWELVE PETALS
Thread 6 white, 1 yellow, back through 1st white,
thread 5 white, back through 6th white,
thread 5 white, 1 yellow, back through 11th white
thread 5 white, back through 16th white, etc.

'ZULU BEADWORK' COLLARS
These are made by Zulus, Ndebele, Xhosa and probably other South African tribes. They are threaded on a honeycomb principle, with an extra strengthening thread around the inner edge, put through right at the end when the fastening is constructed – usually a bead button and loop. This method is also known as 'netting', 'à feston' or 'greenland'. Very often the beads that are threaded through twice to create the lace or net structure are in a contrasting colour which makes threading and counting easier. These African beadwork collars often have characteristic colours of white, light and dark blue, pink, black and red. The old examples used the beautiful red rocailles made with a white core and a transparent rose-red coating, known as 'cornaline d'Aleppo', and the pinks and blues were in tints that are no longer made. We know the beads are at least a hundred years old because those colours are also seen in Victorian bead embroidery.

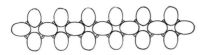

Needle weaving with two threads. Build up a strip with embroidery beads using two independent threads. The second
thread goes through every other bead of the first thread,
adding a new bead between each

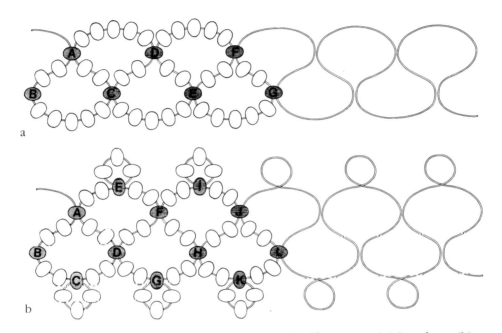

a

b

Basic bead lace pattern (a). Picot loops (b).
(a) The thread follows a regular rhythmic pattern of loops
returning through every third or sixth bead, shown here
shaded.
(b) The basic pattern can be varied and embellished with
additional 'picot' loops as shown

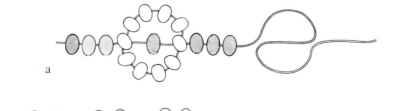

a

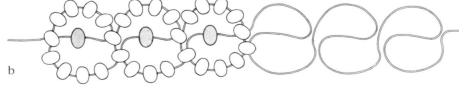

b

Single Daisy (a). Continuous daisies (b). These patterns are
easy to master by following the diagram and are very satisfying even for children to make.

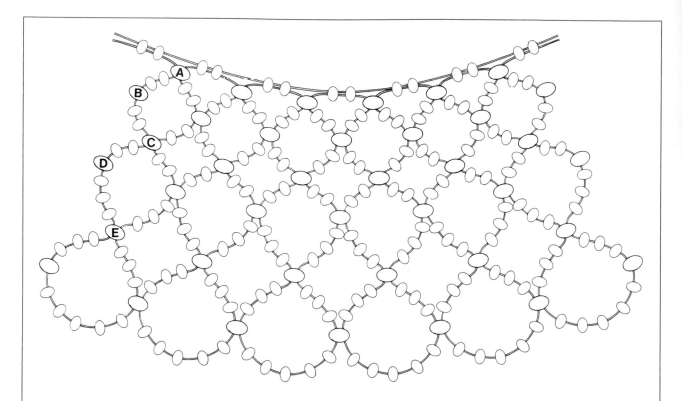

Zulu beadwork collar construction. This is the basic pattern for a curved bead lace 'honeycomb' collar. Like (a) in the picture on page 61 the thread goes from the inside edge down in a zigzag with increasing numbers of beads, making a loop at the bottom and returning, threading the beads in decreasing numbers between each shaded bead towards the inner edge, then back again. When the collar reaches the required length, an additional thread goes through the inner edge to add strength, and attach fastener

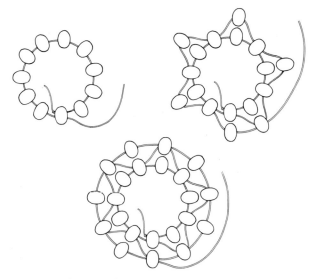

Peyote stitch. To build up a round snake or sausage shape, working spirally, the needle goes through every other bead, adding a new bead between each one

The Ndebele and Xhosa, like the Zulus, also used beads, and they developed a characteristic stitch with which they constructed relatively large flat items of beadwork, even complete 'aprons', as well as using beads stitched onto leather and other materials. The characteristic Ndebele patterns use the same motifs as they paint on their walls and gateways.

The Zulus also make headbands, necklaces, belts and bangles with one or more rolls of plant fibres, leather or cloth, which are tightly wrapped around with beads.

Peyote Stitch

The North American Indians and the Zulus also developed a construction technique to make a patterned sausage shape with beads. Popularly called 'peyote stitch' it is basically a cylindrical honeycomb stitch worked spirally.

Thread 11 beads, back through No 1, thread No 12, back through No 3,
thread 13, back through 5, thread 14, back through 7, thread 15, back through 9, thread 16, back through 11, thread 17, back through 12, thread 18, back through 13, thread 19, back through 14, thread 20, back through 15, thread 21, back through 16, thread 22, back through 17, thread 23, back through 18, thread 24, back through 19, and so on; the ends can fasten with a button and buttonhole of beads, or a barrel shaped screw clasp.

Various antique items of Zulu and Xhosa beadwork – belts, collars, headbands

Sometimes in antique markets you will see long 1920s' snakes worked in beads to give a similar appearance, but using a crochet technique around a core of cord, finished with a stuffed head and pointed tail. Some beautiful examples have dates and initials worked in, which were made by Turkish prisoners of war at the beginning of the century.

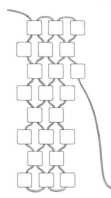

Basic honeycomb construction for trivets. This is worked with regular cylindrical beads

Beaded trivets

The small moulded, very regular cylindrical 'tile beads' or 'cube allies' were made into a honeycomb construction with one continuous thread as teapot stands or little mats. By this method, quite large fabrics of beads could be built up without a loom or framework. Some of the Zulu and Ndebele ornaments of rocaille beads are made with this technique.

The netting construction was also often used to make small Victorian decorative drawstring purses. A tubular shape was made, line by line vertically, and then joined. The top edge was then stitched onto a silk or velvet lining of the same shape, trimmed with a tassel at the bottom where the edges had been gathered together and secured. This shape is sometimes called a 'Dorothy bag', which may not be as old as the shape itself (Judy Garland as Dorothy carries a fabric one in *The Wizard of Oz*). They were also sometimes made around a wooden 'purse mould', a cylindrical solid shape, with the rows being made horizontally or spirally.

BEADWEAVING

This is a well-known, recognisable technique used in Victorian and Edwardian jewellery, usually with evening bags and beaded trimmings. North American Indians and tribes in Kenya have also worked beadweaving in distinctive styles. Small metal or wooden bead looms are on the market and are made to accommodate quite long woven strips, with adjustable

rollers at each end to wind on any extra length, but you can also wind a warp around a cardboard or wooden cigar box, or an old rectangular picture frame, and the result will be just as good. Briefly, the technique is as follows.

There has to be one more warp thread than the number of beads making one row across the width. It is stronger if the edge warps are, in fact, double threads. So, for a strip five beads wide, wind eight warp strands; for a strip ten beads wide, wind thirteen strands. If rocaille beads are used, you should take into account that they are doughnut shaped and not very regular. If you plan a pattern on squared paper it will come out rather elongated.

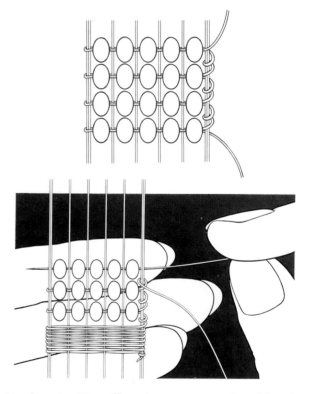

Beadweaving. You will need one more warp thread than the number of beads used to form one row. Make the edge warps stronger by using double thread. If you do not have a metal or wooden bead loom, use a cardboard or wooden cigar box, or even an old rectangular picture frame. For a strip of five beads, wind eight warp strands. Thread a beading needle with a good length of thread, which can be single, and attach the end to one of the warps with an overhand knot. Begin by weaving a few rows in and out. Thread the first row of beads and pass the needle *under* the warps. Raise the beads by pressing them up between the warps with your finger. Take the needle back through the beads *above* the warps and pull the slack weft thread through carefully. This row is now in place. For a firm edge take the thread once round the edge warp on its own. Repeat the process for each row

For the basic weaving technique, thread a beading needle with a good length of thread, as it is difficult to join on new threads and best to avoid having to do so too often. The thread can be a single thread for weaving, and if you wax it from time to time it is less likely to tangle. After attaching the end of the thread to one of the warps with an overhand knot around the warp, you can start by weaving a few rows in and out. Then, to start, put your first complete row of beads onto the weaving thread, pass the needle *under* the warps and then raise the row of beads with your finger pressing the whole row of them up between the warps, each in its position. Thread the needle back through the row of beads *over the top* of the warp threads. Carefully pull through all the slack weft thread. The row is now in place. It is quite advisable every one or two rows to go round the edge warp alone a second time to create a firm edge. Repeat the weaving process for each row.

To join in a new thread, make the join near the middle of the strip, not at the edge, using a weaver's knot which is the most secure (see page 47), provided you can tighten it without interfering with the tension on the beads.

You can make a bracelet or choker to an exact measurement. Make a buttonhole slit a few rows from the end by dividing the warps in the centre and working the two sides independently for a few rows, then stitch on a button at the other end. Stretchy headbands and bracelets can also be constructed with a warp of elastic thread, by adding an extra stitch around the edge with each row, not too tight, to allow for the stretch.

Finishing off

Either your piece can be finished off straight, with the warps paired up, and knotted together, and then, using a needle and one strand at a time, the strands stitched back in and out of one or two rows into the weaving before being trimmed off (the ends can also be glued to the back of a strip of felt or velvet later stitched around the end), or, you can decrease gradually by putting pairs of warp threads together as in the

A buttonhole slit can be worked into the weaving by dividing the warps in the centre and working the two sides independently for a few rows. The button is then stitched on the other end

Beadweaving can be finished off by gradual decreasing, by putting pairs of warp threads together. Start off by threading warps 1, 2 and 3 together and 6, 7 and 8 together for a couple of rows, then take in warp 4 with 1, 2 and 3, and 5 with 6, 7 and 8. Tie the ends with an overhand knot

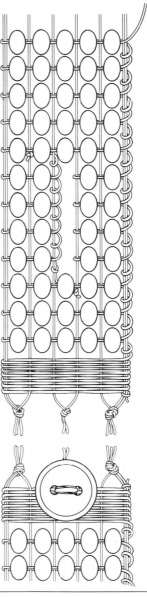

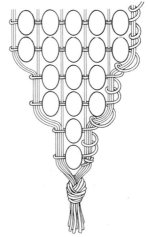

diagram, putting warps 1, 2 and 3, and 6, 7 and 8 together for a few rows, then putting 1, 2, 3, 4 and 5, 6, 7, 8 together until the end. Fabric such as velvet can be stitched along the entire length, with a strip of Velcro to close.

Some long Edwardian necklaces were made with motifs of beadweaving interspersed with lengths of beaded warps – presumably, before warping up, the warp threads would have had all their beads threaded on. The right amount of beads were slid into place and then the next weaving motif made, then more beads slid along and so on. Strips of beadweaving could be stitched together to make larger pieces of beadweaving, such as bead purses and little dainty evening bags, fitted with a fabric lining, a drawstring fastening and trimmed with tassels or fringes.

For belts, a strip of beadweaving can have a row of buttons attached at one end and a row of loops at the other, or each end can be stitched to a manufactured belt fastening. For an adjustable length, each finished end, or the whole length, can be firmly stitched onto a strip of leather with a normal buckle, and the other end with a sequence of holes, or a row of tough ribbons or cords at each end will allow the belt to be tied tighter or looser.

KNITTING AND CROCHET WITH BEADS

This requires the beads to be already on the yarn before the work starts, being passed up one at a time as each stitch is made. The knitting needle or crochet hook does not need to go through the bead, but holes need to be large enough for the yarn. Examples survive from the early nineteenth century, with tiny complicated patterns of flowers and foliage, landscapes and sometimes initials, dates or messages. These must have been worked out on squared paper beforehand, and the beads counted, colour by colour, and row by row. More recently, knitting or crochet in raffia with wood or plastic beads of one colour, or finer cotton with pearl beads, has reappeared at least once in popular fashion for handbags or evening purses, or even the soft hats or caps that envelop the hair, and are called 'snoods'.

No old-fashioned country kitchen was complete without beaded net covers over the milk jug and sugar bowl. A square or circle, slightly larger than the vessel, of muslin or fine cotton cheesecloth or net, was trimmed around the edges with a crochet lace border,

Nineteenth-century beadwork purses

Sixties' plastic bead kitsch, including bead-shaped candle arrangement

'Turkish prisoner-of-war beadwork' snake; with beaded Islamic worry beads and amulets, possibly from Sudan

incorporating characteristic glass beads (jug beads) to weigh it down.

Large-holed beads, held on with a terminal overhand knot, are threaded onto the leather, suede or chamois fringes on the 'Buffalo Bill' cowboy-and-Indian type of jackets, and on skirts, waistcoats, saddlebags and other souvenirs.

BEADED HAIR STYLES

Apart from the tassels on slides, combs and clips, hair can be decorated with beads threaded directly onto the end of narrow plaits. Princesses of the twelfth dynasty in ancient Egypt wore gold-beaded wigs, and the black peoples of Africa have always made wonderful and practical ornamental creations with their hair – in the last decade the beaded look suddenly became fashionable, and was imitated by Western women and men. In order to have hundreds of regular and even-length plaits all over the head, false hair, wool or rags are plaited in. Each narrow plait terminates in one, two, three or more beads, pulled on with a small loop of wire used like a needle threader. To stop the beads sliding off, the end may be held with a small elastic band, or even a milk bottle top, or a blob of candle wax, or two thread ends can be plaited in and knotted around the bottom bead, or a metal crimp squeezed around the end. The whole hairdo may take several hours to create, but once in place remains for weeks or months!

BEADED LIGHT-SWITCH PULLS

The light-switch pull in the bathroom could have a custom finish to harmonise with the colour of the decorations. The pull cords are of nylon braid and can be bought by the metre (yard) from hardware stores. Some pull cords have a metal screw fastener by the switch itself which would allow you to connect in a new cord without an unsightly joining knot. When designing, remember this is a handle so it must be easy to grip and not too heavy and if it swings and hits the wall, must not crack itself or mark the wall.

BEAD CURTAINS

Nowadays bead curtains may be associated with inner doorways of Chinese or Indian restaurants, or questionable massage parlours, but many Victorian and Edwardian homes used to have glass-bead curtains over a hall doorway or a window, bringing an element of colour, movement, light and sparkle. The antique ones I have encountered are of large-holed 'jug beads', threaded rather randomly on parcel string

with knots at intervals, with the string either looped over a dowel or pole at the top, or threaded through drilled holes in a rod with a stop knot (overhand knot), or stitched onto a canvas tape in turn, folded and stitched into a tube which was threaded onto a curtain pole for hanging.

Two curtains which I have made were connected string by string onto runners for a type of patent curtain rail called Swish. I secured the bottom of each string with a callotte over a knot. When working a definite pattern with irregular beads, counting alone will not help you get the pattern right. By starting at the bottom, and threading each complete string, hanging them next to each other as you go, you will be able to align your design. Try to avoid anything very geometric or any straight horizontal lines. Remember also that unlike a window of stained glass, strong light coming through will not glow, so the curtain is more colourful with oblique or reflected light.

VICTORIAN BEADWORK ON CANVAS

As Idalia B. Littlejohns tells us in *Beadcraft:*

> Beads and canvas must be of the right size for one another. If the beads are too small for the canvas (or the canvas too coarse in weave for the beads) the threads of the canvas will be visible between the beads, and if the beads are too large for the canvas (or the canvas too fine in weave for the beads) the canvas cannot possibly lie flat. . . . A medium weave such as Penelope Canvas No. 30 will be the most satisfactory to commence with. . . . Sewing beads onto canvas is a very simple matter. There appear to be only two ways of doing the actual sewing. . . . The first is the upright stitch. Commence at the left hand side of the canvas. Bring the needle and thread up through a hole in the mesh, thread one bead on the needle, and pass the needle down through the hole immediately above, thus making one upright stitch. Now bring the needle up through the hole to the right of the first bead, thread one bead on the needle and pass the needle down through the hole immediately above . . . etc. . . . The second method is a slanting stitch exactly like the first half of a cross stitch.

This gives a diagonal slant in the same direction to each bead, and can often be seen on Victorian beadwork, sometimes combined with 'Berlin woolwork', on chair backs and seats, footstools, under glass on clock stands and tea-trays, fire-screens, purses, handbags and bags, needlecases, etc.

Cleaning

Where the fabric and thread will stand it, gentle washing in lukewarm soapy water followed by a clear rinse will remove grime from glass beads. Otherwise rub over lightly with natural turpentine, surgical spirit, or dry-cleaning fluid with a cloth or soft toothbrush. Do not use solvents to clean artificial or natural pearls, coral, ivory or bone, amber, plastic or opals. If in doubt, stand them in a jam jar containing several spoonfuls of dry potato flour and shake gently.

Save your old nylon socks for washing loose glass beads. Put the beads to be washed inside the sock, and knot the end loosely or close with a rubber band. The beads can then be immersed in soapy water, agitated, rubbed around, and held under the tap to rinse without danger of loss.

BEAD EMBROIDERY

Modern bead embroidery is very free and not so limited to two dimensions, being more like collage with an occasional stitch. It is beyond the scope of my knowledge and experience, and not really fitting in the context of this book. Traditional bead embroidery makes most use of two or three basic stitches. A few beads at a time may be threaded onto the needle, and sewn to the fabric with a stitch similar to a running stitch, sometimes called 'lazy stitch', or you may have a thread with the beads already on, which stays on the right side of the fabric, while a second thread comes up through at intervals and holds it down, like 'couching'.

Commercial beaded dresses, so popular in the twenties and appearing in profusion again in antique costume dealers, as well as modern beaded dresses, are probably all beaded with the use of a tambour hook, which resembles a miniature and lethally sharp crochet hook of steel, set in a wooden handle. The design was mounted on a frame and worked from the back. All the beads were already on the thread and generally of the same colour. The hook was used to pull a loop of the thread through the fabric, followed by another loop, with one bead in between each stitch along the outline of the design, so that only beads would be visible on the right side, while on the back would appear a row of chain stitch. A tambour hook is among the tools illustrated on page 25.

Repairs

In attempting repairs to beadwork or beadweaving you will have to reconstruct the thread fabric itself, starting quite far back into the unbroken area, by attaching a fine new thread somewhere. Inconspicuously between two beads, make a self-tightening overhand knot around a good thread rather than attached to a broken end, then attempt to retrace the path of the original thread. Finish with another small knot around a firm thread. Here it may be justifiable to apply the very smallest possible dot of glue to secure. For these sorts of repairs to African beadwork, do not rule out the use of fine gauge stiff nylon gut. The thread is not going to take much strain and it may make it easier to go in and out of beads more than once, since you won't need a needle. Use a glue like Uhu on the end tucked inside beads, rather than knots.

It is risky to repair canvas beadwork. Once the linen thread of the backing starts to perish, it is difficult to reconstruct a patch with a solid darn as the fibre is ready to disintegrate all over. Until recently, old beadwork was often dismantled as the work to reconstruct seemed greater than the value of the piece itself. Now they are scarcer, this is changing.

7
MAKING BEADS

The following processes and techniques are possible with a simple selection of tools and will augment and vary your range of choice. Although some of these suggested methods of beadmaking are very basic and similar to the earliest techniques, it need not follow that your results will look primitive. No doubt fashion styles and personal taste will influence the kinds of beads you will want to create. Do not try to duplicate beads that are already available from other sources – your efforts are better spent on unusual or exclusive patterns. If you set the trend, you can also name the price.

The techniques described here do not include lapidary skills or working molten glass, which require highly specialised equipment and a professional level of expertise.

To start with there are a variety of objects that already have holes: from pebbles and fossils to small machine parts, cotton reels, door keys, Polo mints, worn seashells, mutton bones, macaroni, and so on. It is not difficult to bore or pierce holes in most seeds, beans, nuts, acorn cups, teeth, claws, shells, bones, pine cones, dried seaweed pods, and small chunks of mother of pearl, wood or ivory. A needle will push through fresh seeds and pips such as melon and apple, and if you can hold the item rigid while working, then even the household hand drill (like an egg beater) or ratchet-drill or primitive bow drill, will be quite efficient, but if you become really interested in making your own beads, it is well worth investing in your own modelmaker's precision hand-held electric drill. It will give you a tremendous freedom as you can hold and control the drill in one hand and, depending on the material, the work in the other hand, enabling you to move about. Suitable drill bits for wood and bone and soft metal are steel high-speed twist drills like the larger ones used in carpentry, but for shell, stone and all hard materials you will need quite a range of 'burrs' including one or two diamond drill bits. In use, lubricate continually with water or spit. If you can, make friends with a dentist, as her or his experience and advice may be useful and you may be able to acquire and prolong the useful life of used drill bits which would otherwise be thrown away.

You can drill gemstones entirely, a long painstaking job, but you will find it uneconomical in quantity as it is so easy and inexpensive to purchase them ready drilled, but beware, the cheapest may be inaccurately drilled. Your drill will be useful to organise, clear, smooth out and enlarge the rougher holes.

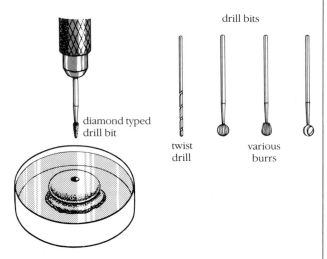

drill bits

diamond typed
drill bit

twist
drill

various
burrs

When using a small precision power drill, support the item to be drilled in a clamp or on a piece of Blu-tack, in a small container filled with water to cover it

DRILLING

To use a small precision power drill: wood, shell, bone, plastic, pearl, etc. can be held in the hand while drilling. With the hardest substances (glass, stone, crystal) it is a safe standard practice to support the item in some kind of clamp, or cushion it on a lump of Blu-tack on a flat hard surface, even within a small container that can be filled up with water to cover the bead. The water helps as a lubricant and cooling agent, and prevents rapid clogging of the drill. Keep withdrawing the drill to get rid of extra grindings.

From outside: long beads of brown glass, blown by the author, threaded with round brown and blue glass beads. Necklace of Indian glass beads, tumbled to give a matt surface texture, knotted and twisted on assembled cord, with adjustable sliding bead fastening

Where the two half-holes meet crookedly inside a bead there may be a sharp inside edge and a 'corner in the tunnel'. Careful and gradual pressure with a small-diameter diamond drill bit will smooth out the rough inside edges. Too much continuous pressure though may result in a snapped-off drill bit securely wedged in the aperture.

TUMBLING

Another interesting piece of equipment to experiment with is a stone tumbler, available from lapidary suppliers. A small motor rotates one or two containers, which hold your stones with water and progressively finer 'grits', and over a period of time the stones become more smooth, polished and eventually shiny. You can follow the instructions that come with the kit for polishing up stones, or use the second finest grit only for just a few hours with cheap semi-precious beads or rather boring or chipped glass beads to take the high gloss off, resulting a matt or frosted finish with a wonderful tactile appeal. Broken glass beads with holes intact can take on a new identity if tumbled like this to take off the jagged edges.

WOOD

Wood and bone can be whittled, filed and sandpapered without sophisticated tools and skills, but you might find you become interested in woodturning on a miniature lathe. There are a number of enthusiasts now making lace bobbins and other forms of 'treen' – small-scale turned wood articles using the same techniques. With beads, the hole would be drilled last.

TUBES

There are all kinds of materials available in the form of hollow tubes or tubing, which can probably be cut into sections with an old toothed bread knife, a hacksaw or jeweller's saw. Metal, bamboo, reed, hollow chicken bones, macaroni, hollow twigs, drinking straws, empty felt-pen holders of all colours, coloured rubber or plastic hose, pencils with their leads pushed out, coloured electric cable with wire extracted, and even long tubular glass beads can be sectioned by filing a groove then breaking smartly.

MODELLING

Modelling involves working with a soft pliable material which is later hardened. It will be much easier to work in traditional clay if you have access to raw materials and a kiln, so it is very useful if you can join a local class or enrol for a weekend course once or twice a year, but there are also now a variety of modelling compounds on the market that need no firing. If the opportunity arises try using straight earthenware to experiment with shapes and try the effects of stoneware, raku, porcelain with body colour, coloured and lustre glazes, sawdust firing and Egyptian paste or faience.

Egyptian paste

Here is a very simple recipe for Egyptian paste, which will make enough beads for a necklace. You will need access to a kiln, so ask your pottery teacher for advice. Exact amounts are not critical.

16 level dsp powdered flint or quartz
4 level dsp bentonite
2 level dsp sodium bicarbonate
½ level dsp copper carbonate to give typical turquoise blue colouring, or cobalt oxide for lapis blue, chromium oxide for green and manganese oxide for greys, browns or mauves
NB Do not use kitchen utensils for copper carbonate, and wash hands well after use, as it can be toxic.

Mix ingredients well together then add water until mixture is malleable. Model into simple small beads – it is not easy to make anything other than simple shapes.

Because the mixture contains its own glaze it only needs one firing, but the outer surface must not be touched once the beads have been modelled. So, after modelling, support the beads in the positions in which they will be fired and leave to dry slowly. Then fire at a temperature of 860-950°C (1592-1742°F).

More recipes can be found in the *Illustrated Dictionary of Practical Pottery* by Robert Fournier.

Enormous quantities of tiny delicate cylindrical faience beads were made by the ancient Egyptians and stitched into complex collars and beadwork 'nets'. According to research by Mary Seyd, these were made by dipping short lengths of dried grass into the faience paste, which was made to a liquid consistency. The grasses were then stuck upright into the base of a newly modelled clay saucer and a similar clay lid was lowered on top (the clay would have been firm but not dry). This would then be left to dry in the sun before firing. During firing, the paste would fuse and the grass turn to ash, leaving hollow rods attached to the protective base. The base would be broken away when cool.

Whatever clay (or other substance) you use, model your beads by the set, and always make a few more than you plan to use so that you can pick out the best ones. For round or disc shapes such as those used in Project 2, divide your modelling material into more than the required number of equal-sized rounds (roughly 'petits pois' size). For small round beads they can just be rolled between the fingers, pierced with a cocktail stick or knitting needle, and left to dry thoroughly. (Wet clay or glazed beads dry easily if left on a cocktail stick stuck upright into a potato.) For discs and other shapes, larger clay rounds can be rolled, pinched or squashed before being pierced.

When soft, any modelled beads can be given a texture by pressing or rolling them onto the surfaces of files, graters, rubber stamps with lettering, leaves, coarse fabric and so on.

Papier maché

This is simply soaked newspaper torn up very small and mixed with wallpaper paste. It shrinks and hardens when dry. Pierce with a cocktail stick or knitting needle. Beads of papier maché are very light. In China and Japan, papier maché beads were heavily lacquered and sometimes inlaid with tiny pieces of mother-of-pearl, shell, coral, metal or turquoise.

Playdough

To a cupful of flour add 2 tbsp salt and just enough water to make a stiff paste. Pierce the beads with a cocktail stick or knitting needle, and dry over a radiator. This mixture may swell slightly as it dries.

Gesso or plaster

Gesso is an old-fashioned but durable mixture of whiting and glue or size. Plaster of Paris or a filling plaster (available from DIY stores) can be used for similar results, but sets more quickly. Dried plaster beads are absorbent and can be painted and varnished, or saturated with fragrant oils for scented beads.

Rosepetal paste

Thoroughly mashed rosepetals left in the sun for a few days can also be used as a modelling paste. The resulting beads will resemble carved wood with a trace of the scent of roses which can be enhanced when dry by the addition of a few drops of oil of roses. (Pippa Fog specialises in turning customers' wedding bouquets into romantic necklaces, interspersing the rosepetal beads with Venetian glass beads with rosebud decoration.)

Commercial modelling compounds

Handicraft shops also sell various self-hardening modelling clays under different names such as Barbola, Plastone, Cold Clay and Das. Follow the manufacturer's instructions in each case.

Fimo is a coloured modelling compound formulated to harden permanently when brought to a low heat in the oven for a short time. It comes in little packets of each colour, with exact instructions. Colours can be mixed, embedded and rolled, or marbled together, for interesting effects.

PAPIER ROULÉ

Rolled paper beads may be made by cutting quality colour magazines, bookbinding or wrapping paper into long triangular strips which are coated, after the first 12mm (½in) at the wide end, with wallpaper paste and then rolled tightly round a knitting needle or cocktail stick making a long oval or torpedo shape, as illustrated. When dry they can be varnished for extra strength and durability. Choose to cut a

Papier roulé beads are made by cutting suitable quality paper into long triangular strips. Coat each strip with wallpaper paste starting 12mm (½in) in from the straight side with wallpaper paste, and rolling it tightly around a cocktail stick or knitting needle to form a torpedo shape. Leave the bead to dry before varnishing

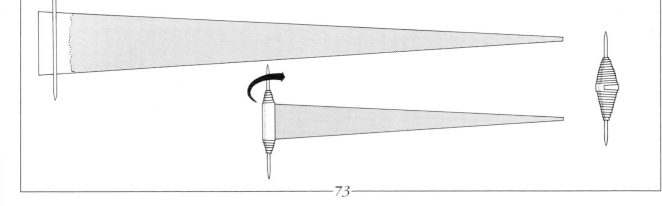

(a) A beaded bead is a plain wooden bead that is covered with tiny embroidery beads to create an attractive colourful effect. The surface is worked in segments like slices of orange peel.

Thread a beading needle with a long piece of single thread. Thread through the large bead once and tie to secure, pulling the knot inside the hole. Now thread up through the bead, add enough embroidery beads to cover the distance down to the hole at the opposite end. Thread up through again, and a second time through the first two embroidery beads already on the first loop. Add new beads to lie alongside the first strand as shown, but thread again through the two last beads of the first loop. Return up through the centre again and repeat, resulting in a segment shape. Now start a new segment next to the first one and repeat till the surface is covered. Be sure to pull the thread tight each time. Experiment by varying the colours.

(b) The birdcage bead is a grooved glass bead with a row of embroidery beads threaded to rest in each groove

Turk's head knots in leather and paper (a). Crocheted button (b). Corn dolly bead (c). Beads can be built up from thread or thong in various ways, including the good solid Turk's head knot worked in a double strand of round leather thong, or a strip of paper, fabric or grass. The crocheted button makes a useful bead and even the corn dolly braiding techniques will make an original and decorative threadable shape

When using a flat stone or similar object for a pendant, stick one or two loops to the back of the object with a strong glue such as Araldite (a). For other shapes, such as a pear-shaped pebble, drill a small hole in the top of the object and glue in a wire shank to attach the thread (b)

matching set from pages where the whole picture is in related tones of one or two colours. Papier roulé beads are used in Project 2.

METALWORKING (SILVERSMITHING)

As with pottery you will have a great advantage if you are able to join a class, as so many of the tools and equipment are expensive and specialised. If you are relentless about your enterprise there are, however, some possibilities even at home.

Metal tubing is easy to cut with a hacksaw, and rough edges can be smoothed with files and 'wet and dry' Carborundum abrasive paper.

Most wire can be used like fibre and will stand being knitted, crocheted, knotted, braided, made into cord with an old-fashioned knitting dolly, and, combined in this way, with beads. For inspiration see *Textile Techniques in Metal* by Arline M. Fisch.

At a class you would learn casting, repoussé, enamelling, chasing pierced designs, filigree, etching, anodising and oxidising to colour metal, and a whole term could be usefully devoted to experimenting in making interesting fasteners and catches if you were to become really fanatical. Some designers incorporate their trademark on a specially made fastening.

APPLIED DECORATION

Any of the cheaper beads can be embellished in various ways by painting, or even collage.

Unvarnished wood can be dyed with cold water dyes (following the manufacturer's instructions for dyeing by hand), or decorated with felt pens or paint and then varnished. A pattern can be burnt on with a red-hot needle, or an electric pyrography tool available from craft suppliers. Cold enamels, gold leaf and sealing wax can also be used to create colour and pattern. Or the bead can be coated with glue (eg Uhu) and a collage built up using pressed flowers, fabrics, glitter, sequins, or flock.

A plain spherical wooden bead can be completely covered with tiny embroidery beads to make a beaded bead, or a 'birdcage' bead can be made with strands of tiny beads around a grooved glass bead (see illustrations).

Epoxy resin (eg Araldite, normal or rapid) is a very useful and versatile glue which has volume as well as great sticking power. It can be put to various uses including adding a loop to turn a small object into a pendant, as shown in the illustration.

Felt, leather and other fabrics can be used as discs threaded between other beads to help prevent abrasion and add a different decorative element.

Necklaces of natural coloured substances.
From outside: fine hand-painted wooden beads by Sue
Lyness; beads covered in reptile leather; hand-made lami-
nated ivory, tortoiseshell and inlaid leather beads by
Malcolm Logan; laminated inlay beads of exotic woods by
Edwin Spencer

8
DESIGN

Design is so personal and subjective that I was reluctant to define, let alone impose, aesthetic criteria of any sort, and as fashions and epochs change so do the standard definitions of 'good' and 'bad' taste. However, there are in fact a number of necessary and practical design guidelines that apply to threading beads, regardless of the fashionable trends of the day.

DESIGN ARRANGEMENT

Unless you deliberately intend to make the necklace look awkward as it hangs, there are some simple suggestions which will help you design something that looks right. Patterns for necklace sequences may be symmetrical (or intentionally assymmetrical), processional or repeating, or seemingly random.

Symmetrical
This means both sides more or less the same, or at any rate in balance, with a definite heavy or important bead in the centre, and other subsidiary beads paired up along the sides in reducing sizes. If a symmetrical necklace is long enough and intended to go around more than once, remember that the fastener may then appear at the front. You must decide whether to have one or two larger beads there, or put the fastener at the side.

Processional or repeating
By processional I mean an even pattern unit that repeats its sequence along the entire length of the necklace without its having a centre, which is suitable for long chains that can be looped around several times. Sizes can be mixed, larger and smaller, but the overall impression of the necklace should be kept more or less regular all the way along. The pattern unit that repeats could itself be symmetrical. For long rhythmical sequences like these that will get a lot of wear, it is a good idea for safety reasons to include knots, if only once or twice in each repeat, to minimise the loss of beads if the thread breaks.

Assymetrical
At times, fashion emphasises the assymetrical – clothes button up at one side or cross over, a dress bares one shoulder, hair is swept to one side, single earrings are worn – but an off-centre necklace is very difficult to design. For one thing, any important heavy bead will try to slide down to the front, wherever you may place it, unless you either fix it additionally with a brooch pin, or cunningly balance up the rest of the necklace by weight. Experiment on loose thread first. This effect is sometimes achieved with multistrand graduated pearls in order to allow a beautiful clasp to show at the side as a feature.

Random
A collection of interesting individual beads will thread up into a pleasing necklace without any symmetry or imposed repeating sequence if there is a relating theme of one or two colours, and the sizes are fairly compatible. Select your favourites and arrange them at close intervals to be at the front, with plainer ones between to allow them to stand out. If individual beads are highly decorated or patterned, space them out with plainer ones between. If you have a whole sequence of heavily decorated beads the effect will be very concentrated, dense and rich, without allowing the beads to be seen individually.

Colour
As with clothes and make-up, bead jewellery needs to tone with the eyes, hair and skin colours. Unlike clothing, which covers a large area, a necklace can be more vivid in itself without looking too brash as it may provide a small but intense accent to liven up a single 'understated' outfit. In fact it will disappear unless it is positive and bright. I believe that you need not stick to one colour or even one or two tints or mixtures close to each other in the spectrum, but to keep the necklace as an identifiable unity you should start with one main colour which should predominate, repeated positively to maintain the theme, and then one or two subsidiary colours or neutrals (clear, cream, grey, beige, brown, flesh colour, small metals beads or black) repeating between. White in this context is not a neutral colour. To my taste, for example, turquoise tones well with dark jasper green and grey, or coral with white and golden brown.

Not every single spectrum colour exists in natural

materials or in glass. Among the gemstones that are made into beads you will not find a natural fuchsia pink or cerise, or lemon yellow nor a strong purple, indigo or navy, although these colours are sometimes created for fashion's sake by staining calcite, shell or mother-of-pearl. In glass, too, it is difficult to find certain colours as beads such as ruby red, rose pink, violet, mauve, purple, navy blue and real grey. One reason is that some of the oxides used in smelting to colour the glass are extremely expensive. The rose colour is made with an oxide of gold, for example. Except when the quirks of fashion dictate otherwise, good true yellows and greens may be hard to find as they do not normally sell very well, except to Japanese! None of these problems exists with plastic, wooden beads, or fake pearls which can be dyed like nylon to any shade of the moment but will never stop looking cheap, in my opinion, and may fade.

It is fun to design a necklace to match a dress for a special occasion. If the fabric is a plain colour you are completely free to choose a harmonising or contrasting colour, or even the same colour but perhaps shiny, sparkly or brighter, depending on the other accessories – shoes, handbag, belt, hat – and other jewellery. If the fabric has a strong pattern it is more tricky to create a necklace that will stand out. Generally, make it a short necklace or a choker so that it shows on your skin not on top of the fabric. It is not difficult to make a long one that will disappear as if camouflaged! Do not introduce another colour but pick one from the pattern – either the background colour or one of the stronger colours in the pattern – as the main colour for the necklace.

PRACTICAL FACTORS

The first design restriction from a practical point of view is weight. To put it simply, very heavy beads will hurt your neck. Where it may be fine to pose for a portrait, sit at a board meeting or have a candlelit dinner in a string of enormous stones, it is definitely not possible to wear them in normal daily activities. The same applies to very grand earrings, although the screws or clips for non-pierced ears may pull less than wires looped through them. Some large beads that are surprisingly light include amber, wood, horn, plastic of course, and hollow metal.

The Egyptians solved the weight problem by completing their necklaces with a heavy counterweight at the back, which reflected or continued the symbolic significance of the main design. Although I personally dislike the idea of being generous with beads at the front where it shows and mean round the back, since a necklace ought to look just as attractive off as on, any

short necklace intended to fit under a shirt collar has to allow for the shirt – only about 8 or 10cm (3 or 4in) at the front will be clear, the other 30cm (12in) at least is going to be covered by clothing and must be discreet. If the back beads are bulky they will stick into you when you put on a coat.

Cylindrical beads
Very long cylindrical beads or long beads with extra large holes articulate awkwardly unless you want the 'off register' effect. Otherwise use a round bead in between each, like a ball and socket joint. A large cylindrical or long oval bead hangs askew if used as the centre bead of a long necklace, and should either be the centre of a short choker, 51cm (20in) or less, or hang vertically as a pendant. Otherwise use any longer beads in pairs either side of a short or round centre bead.

Designing with a pendant
A necklace designed around a pendant will hang in a basic V shape. If the pendant is small, for example a piece from an earring, make the necklace slightly shorter and dainty using only small beads so that it doesn't look out of proportion, or make the pendant appear larger or longer by adding one or two beads, or a tassel. Do not dwarf it with very big beads up the sides. The most impressive and pleasing pendant necklaces reach down to the solar plexus, approximately 86cm (34in).

Two-holed components
Sometimes odd units can be used which are really pieces from old bracelets, beautiful slices of agate, jasper, onyx, ivory or jet, for instance, with two parallel holes. Feature them linking two short strands horizontally as a 'spacer' or vertically threaded with two strands dangling beneath, which could themselves terminate with drop-shaped pendants. Pieces of this sort have been used in Project 3 to create a bracelet and matching earrings.

'SIGNIFICANCE'

When creating a design you also need to consider its significance to the wearer. As well as being an adornment, any piece of jewellery is probably also a souvenir and a personal memento, to evoke a person, place, moment or occasion, and reveals something about you to the world. The colours themselves may have meanings connected with personal or tribal loyalties, or they may represent national or team colours, and it is these associations which may be

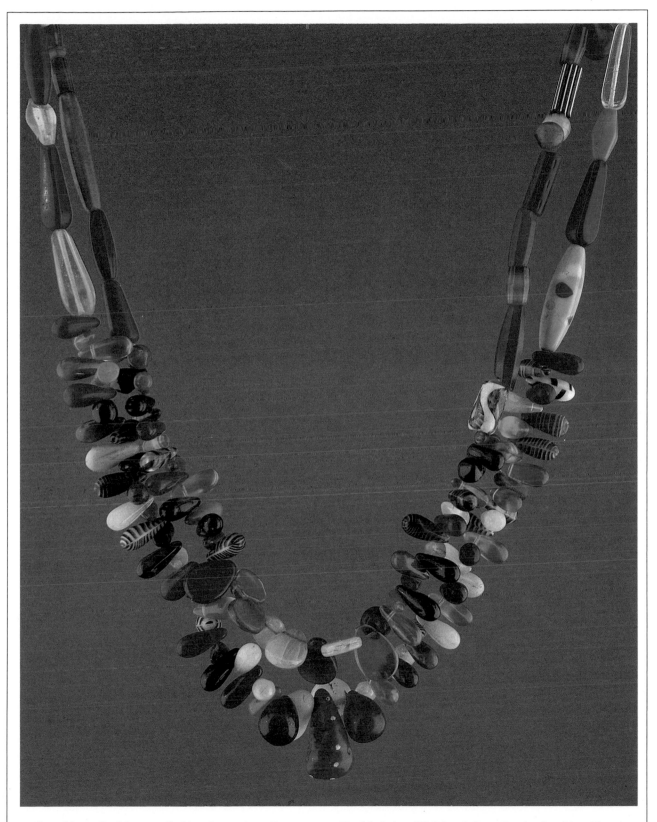

Left: necklace of gold, enamelled beads, pearls, and precious stones by Fred Rich, 1986 (Photo: Fred Rich)

Moulded glass 1930s beads from Czechoslovakia, with a rare Mauritanian Kiffa bead at the centre.

more important than choosing something to suit a person's colouring. For a list of colours and their meanings see the table of colours on page 124.

Putting more emphasis on personal choice, most people have an intuitive affinity with some precious stone which is simple and direct, and needs no explanation (otherwise consult lists of zodiac stones, and stones of the month on page 124.) According to alternative or holistic healing systems, a patient may be told to wear some stone particularly as an aid to restore her or his inward balance, and there are many beliefs connected with gemstones and their possible protective qualities. A gemstone bead on a cord may even be chosen as a dowsing pendulum.

Collections of small charms, or unusual items such as keys, toys, even coloured plastic cracker charms, may create an amusing and decorative necklace, and once you free yourself from the limitations of 'good taste' you can be as outrageous as you like by stringing up teeth, claws, horns, snail shells, chicken bones, tiny animal skulls, snake vertebrae, recycled odds and ends such as canned-drink pulls, rubbers, safety pins, slices of hosepipe and so on. Your necklace will certainly be bizarre, unique, provocative, and may be taken even as a political statement!

Even in ancient Egypt jewellery sometimes included beads from other parts of the world and from earlier periods – those items of former times must have been valued and admired for their intrinsic beauty not despised as old-fashioned. So it is still today. We are impressed by the best feats of the craftsperson and the engineer for some of the amazingly fine, exact, pieces of jewellery that they have made over the last two thousand years. Whether we admire the matchless settings of diamonds in gold and platinum, the baffling techniques of granulation of the Etruscans, or extraordinary miniature oriental carvings, holograms, or micro-electronic flashing 'jewels', we have still not thrown out the charming, simple and often also awesome and stunning jewellery of primitive peoples and extinct civilisations. Perhaps this is because next to our appetite for technical brilliance we also have a very deep-seated intuitive need for those ornaments of inexact beauty but living impact, often charged with generations and even centuries of human warmth and contact.

PROJECTS

This series of seven projects enables you to produce your own attractive jewellery, while learning the several basic skills required. Most of these techniques are more fully described in Chapters 3 and 4 with detailed step-by-step diagrams, so use those chapters as a reference throughout the projects.

If you live in or near a market town you can collect interesting beads of various types from stalls, charity shops, junk dealers and real antique shops, where old beads and broken necklaces can be gathered for a modest outlay – it is a good idea to make frequent and regular visits. In the country you can forage for beads in jumble sales, car-boot and garage sales or small auctions of surplus 'tat'. Passing the word around may bring donations of unexpected treasures. Beads can be made as described in Chapter 7, and many suppliers produce a catalogue and sell by mail order. Some may even offer quantity discounts, but I advise an initial phone call. For a postal enquiry of any sort, do not expect a reply unless you include a *stamped* self-addressed envelope. You will be able to purchase Indian or Czech modern moulded or wound glass beads, as well as petal shapes, smooth coloured wood beads, tiny embroidery beads, coral twigs, mother-of-pearl and semi-precious stone beads and tumbled baroque pebble-shaped chips, and, if you like to use them, plastic beads of all kinds from most suppliers.

For the projects I also used odd old bracelet components with two parallel holes, a few charming antique rosebud-decorated Venetian glass beads, and a good-sized drop-shaped pendant of rose quartz along with a few rose-quartz beads. All these items were typical booty from one visit to a large regular antique market. When dealers get to know you they will save likely looking bits and pieces. Beads that may seem boring or vulgar by themselves may still work when combined as components of an attractive whole.

Project 2 uses hand-made paper beads and beads of coloured low-temperature hardening modelling compound, which can also be used to make feature beads for some of the other projects. Projects 4 and 7 will take a lot of time to thread and complete, so be prepared for long and patient hours. Try to prevent your threads from tangling, and trust that though the techniques may seem tricky at first, with patience you will achieve beautiful and perfect necklaces. Hopefully, once the skills are mastered and you have some personal experience with what beads and thread can do, you will be able to vary and invent a design according to whatever treasures you may make or find.

RED THONG CHOKER

This simple choker, made from glass and wooden beads, has an adjustable sliding fastening.

Materials
1m (39in) round red thong
12 10mm (²/₅in) round red wood beads with sufficiently large holes
2 8mm round red wood beads
10 large-holed Indian wound glass cylinders, 15mm (³/₅in) long
3 large-holed Indian wound round swirly beads, 15mm (³/₅in) diameter
1 small plain red Indian glass bead, 8mm (⁵/₁₆in) diameter, with hole the right size for both ends of thong to fit in tightly

Thread the sequence with the smaller wood beads at each end, glass and wood beads alternating, with one of the large round beads in the centre. Slide the 36cm (14in) of beads towards the centre of the thong length, so the uncovered 'tails' are of equal length. Tie an overhand knot snug against each end of the sequence. Push the two ends together through the smaller red glass bead, and finish each end with a tightened overhand knot. To put it on, slide the red bead to the ends to enlarge the loop, and, when on, tighten to desired length.

Project 1 Red thong choker made from glass and wooden beads
Project 4 Multistrand plaited necklace of pearl beads, moulded shapes and red beads, with matching brooch

2
SIMPLE NECKLACE
with Matching Earrings

This simple 56cm (22in) threaded necklace with earrings uses hand-made beads and a pierced screw fastener (see page 86).

Materials

1m (39in) doubled 40 thread, with wire needle
1 screw fastener without loops
1 pair eyepins and earring fittings
10 long papier roulé beads (4cm/1½in), made as described on page 73
2 short papier roulé beads (2cm/¾in), as above
22 red-brown modelled discs, 16-20mm (⁷⁄₁₀-³⁄₄in) diameter, made from Fimo (see page 72)
9 black modelled discs, 5-8mm (¼-²⁄₅in) diameter, made from Fimo
24 small round modelled turquoise beads, made from Fimo

Tie a secure overhand knot at the end of the doubled thread with the wire needle already attached. Cut end fairly close to knot. Come out through the long half of the fastener as described on page 30, and thread your sequence of beads: 1 small turquoise, papier roulé, turquoise, red-brown, black and red-brown discs, turquoise, papier roulé, etc. to end. Thread into the second half of the fastener, take up the slack and tie an overhand knot as securely as you can. Tighten by pulling the two strands in opposite directions. Cut off 'whiskers'.

MATCHING EARRINGS

Using eyepins, thread 1 turquoise, 1 red-brown, 1 black, red-brown disc, 1 short papier roulé, 1 more turquoise, bend top end into loop as described on page 53 and attach earring fasteners.

3
TWO-STRAND BRACELET
with Earrings

This two-strand bracelet uses crimps and tigertail, with antique two-holed bracelet pieces and embroidery beads, and there is a pair of festooned earrings to match (see page 91). (The other bracelets illustrated are made by the same method.)

Materials

2-strand silver-colour box snap (3-strand could be used if necessary, by omitting to use the centre loop)
2 x 30cm (12in) length tigertail cable
4 silver-colour crimps
7 faceted French jet bracelet pieces with 2 holes
28 small faceted black glass beads (mine came from a twenties bead-embroidered dress decoration)
Tiny black lustre embroidery beads
for the earrings:
2 more bracelet pieces, 20 faceted black beads, and embroidery beads as above

In case you have to adjust the length at each end, it is advisable not to fix the fastener until the whole is threaded, so start with a piece of sellotape folded double over the ends of tigertail temporarily to prevent any beads from sliding off. Be sure to align all the flat pieces and the fastener the right way up. Working 'in parallel' start both strands with a crimp, then 1 embroidery bead, 1 faceted bead, 1 embroidery bead, on each, then they both go through the first bracelet piece;* then 1 embroidery, 1 faceted, 1 embroidery, 1 faceted, 1 embroidery, on each, then go through the next bracelet piece, and repeat that sequence from *, to the last bracelet piece, after which each strand will have 1 embroidery bead, 1 faceted, 1 embroidery bead and then the final crimp. When you are satisfied with the length, about 18cm (7in), thread one end of the tigertail through one loop of the fastener and back

through the crimp and the last few beads. Using snipe-nosed pliers, squash the crimp flat and firm close to the fastener so it grips. Repeat for the second strand at this end. Now remove the sellotape and attach in the same way at the other end, but pull out any extra slack before squashing the crimp. (You can get a grip on the protruding end of tigertail with the snipe-nosed pliers to do this effectively.) Cut off the excess tigertail carefully to avoid scratchy ends using wire cutters.

EARRINGS

These are made with all the 'festoons' on one continuous thread, which loops five times through the two holes in the bracelet piece.

For each earring: using approximately 1m (39in) doubled black 40 thread, with temporary knot (see page 36), thread 4 embroidery beads, 1 faceted, 4 embroidery, 1 faceted, 4 embroidery, 1 faceted, 3 embroidery beads, through earring loop, 3 more embroidery beads, back through last faceted bead, 4 embroidery, 1 faceted, 4 embroidery, 1 faceted, 4 embroidery, down through one hole of bracelet piece, then the festoons are made with graded sizes of loops with a faceted bead at the centre bottom of each:

10 embroidery, 1 faceted, 10 embroidery, *up* through second hole of bracelet piece, across top without beads, *down* through first hole of bracelet piece, 15 embroidery, 1 faceted, 15 embroidery, *up* through, across and *down* as above, 20 embroidery, 1 faceted, 20 embroidery, *up* through, across and *down*, 25 embroidery, 1 faceted, 25 embroidery, *up* through, across and *down*, 30 embroidery, 1 faceted, 30 embroidery, *up* through second hole as before, but now undo temporary knot, tie a secure overhand knot to unite the beginning and end, making sure all the slack has been pulled through, cut off and singe to finish.

4
MULTISTRAND NECKLACE
with Brooch

Various beads are used for this multistrand plaited necklace, approximately 45cm (18in); grey pearl beads, moulded red 'petal' and 'prong' shapes, and small red beads. They are attached with callottes, and there is an attractive brooch to match (see page 83).

Materials
3-strand clasp (diamanté fish-hook type)
Oval brooch template and base
12 callottes, silver colour
At least 150g (6oz) grey 5mm (⅕in) pearl beads
At least 25g (1oz) red 3mm (⅛in) round beads
At least 100g (4oz) each of red 'petal' and 'prong' shapes, or similar

As shown in the illustration, using 1m (39in) lengths of *doubled* 40 thread, thread 6 × 56cm (22in) strands in turn, each with a slightly different repeating combination of shapes:
1. plain grey round pearls
2. grey round, 2 prongs, grey round, 2 prongs . . .
3. grey round, red round, grey round, red prong, repeated . . .
4. grey round, petal, grey round, petal . . .

5. plain round reds
6. grey round, petal, grey round, prong . . .

Pair them as shown in the illustration, and knot one end of each pair with an overhand knot of the 4 strands together, leaving at least 15cm (6in) tail at the end. Attach callotte as on page 34 onto the overhand knot. Knot the other ends *temporarily* together. Attach the 3 callottes with pairs of strands to the 3 holes on one half of the fastener. Start to plait the pairs of strands. It may be helpful to hold this end down with a pin in the workbench, or attach it to something with a safety pin. When plaiting nears completion, you can adjust lengths. The temporary knots make it possible to do this as, when undone, extra beads may be slipped off. Now make your final overhand knots with each pair, attach callottes and attach to other half of fastener. When you are satisfied with the tightness and appearance of your plait, trim off any protruding whiskers.

BROOCH
This is made as described on page 56. The outer ring has alternating prongs and petals, the middle is 9 grey pearl rounds, the centre is 5 petals.

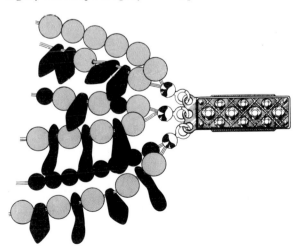

(left) Project 2 Simple threaded necklace using hand-made papier roulé and modelled beads, with earrings
Project 5 Coral twig and embroidery bead necklace, with earrings

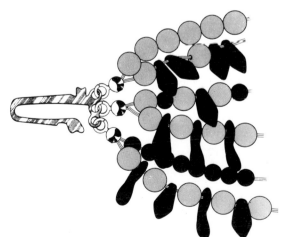

A multistrand plaited necklace of pearl beads, moulded petal and prong shapes and small beads. Once you have paired the six repeated combinations attach each pair of threads to the callottes and split ring before attaching to the three-row fastener

5
CORAL NECKLACE
with Earrings

Coral twigs and small embroidery beads are used to make a pretty necklace, 60cm (24in), and matching earrings (see page 86).

Materials

1m (39in) doubled 40 thread, either black or coral orange
Gilt bolt ring with split ring
2 6mm (¼in) lengths of medium gilt gimp
At least 10g (½oz) (small container) lustre embroidery beads
171 small coral twigs, approximately sorted: 33 larger, 66 medium, 72 smaller
Pair of eyepins and earring wires

Thread the sequence, starting and finishing with the 'Gimp' technique fully described on pages 36-8.

Sequence: 5 embroidery beads, 5 coral twigs (small, medium, large, medium, small) 31 times to end, finishing with 5 embroidery beads.

EARRINGS

Thread onto eyepin: 1 embroidery bead, 1 small coral twig, 1 medium coral twig, a large coral twig, 2 medium coral twigs, 1 small coral twig, 7 embroidery beads, 3 small coral twigs, 3 embroidery beads. Bend the end carefully into a closed loop, using round-nosed pliers as described on page 53, and attach to the earring wire.

6
THREE KNOTTED NECKLACES

This project shows three variations of knotting between beads, creating superb necklaces from beautiful and precious beads. The knotting contributes to the design and makes each bead look special, as well as protecting the beads. It also helps them to hang and move more attractively (see page 91).

LAPIS LAZULI AND CRYSTAL NUGGETS CHOKER

Materials
22 old round lapis beads, their sizes graduated between 15mm (½in) and 8mm (⅖in)
23 irregular natural crystal chunks
1 silver bolt ring and split ring
6 strands of lapis-blue 40 thread (ie 3 doubled through the needle)

Allow a thread length from needle to temporary knot of 152cm (60in). No gimp is used for this necklace as the combined thread is too thick, so the double ring hitch knot (see page 42) is used for the fastener.

Arrange your beads in their graduated sizes, alternately, starting and finishing with a crystal. The necklace is threaded and knotted in the standard way (see pages 39-41), with the final knot tucked inconspicuously between the last crystal and lapis bead.

FRESHWATER PEARLS AND AGATE

This long elegant strand 90cm (36in) of pearl and palest grey can be looped around the neck more than once but has a distinguished yet discreet style.

Materials
95 freshwater pearls drilled across, not along the length
96 of the 4mm (⁵⁄₃₂in) small round grey lace agates.
Delicate silver-filigree box snap, with matching gimp
100cm (39in) doubled 60 thread
White 40 thread, 274cm (108in) when doubled.

To work cleanly you can first thread the entire sequence of alternating pearls and agates, and the gimps at each end, onto the doubled 60 thread. Then remove the needle without cutting the thread, and loop through the white 40 thread and carefully transfer the gimps and beads by sliding them across (see page 47). Now, attach the fastener, and knot carefully between each bead in the usual way.

UNUSUAL ANTIQUE-BEAD NECKLACE AND EARRINGS

This 65cm (26in) necklace incorporates Chinese antique bone beads pierced and carved in a delightful lacy pattern, with mother-of-pearl ovals and regular round beads of an unusual swirly tiger's-eye variation. It is knotted between every three beads with variegated coloured threads to give a matching coloured knot, and there are earrings to match.

Materials
5 larger 14cm (½in) and 10 smaller 8mm (³⁄₁₆in) carved bone beads with large holes
16 antique mother-of-pearl oval beads, 10mm (³⁄₈in), with large holes
22 8mm (⁵⁄₁₆in) and 34 5mm (³⁄₅in) fancy tiger's-eye beads
2 heart-shaped tiger's-eye pendants
Gilt gimp
Bolt ring and split ring
Pair of eyepins
Bails and kidney wires, or earring fittings as preferred
6 strands of 40 thread – 1 each – doubled, of mustard, brown, deep red and black – 152cm (60in) from needle to temporary knot

Thread this sequence:
1 small tiger's-eye, 1st mother-of-pearl, 2 small tiger's-eye,
1st small bone, 2 small tiger's-eye, 2nd mother-of-pearl, 2 small tiger's-eye,
2nd small bone, 2 small tiger's-eye, 3rd mother-of-pearl, 2 small tiger's-eye,
3rd small bone, 2 small tiger's-eye, 4th mother-of-

pearl, 2 small tiger's-eye,
4th small bone, 2 small tiger's-eye, 5th mother-of-pearl, 2 large tiger's-eye,
5th small bone, 2 large tiger's-eye, 6th mother-of-pearl, 2 large tiger's-eye,
1st large bone, 2 large tiger's-eye, 7th mother-of-pearl, 2 large tiger's-eye,
2nd large bone – this is the centre bead. Repeat in reverse order to end.

Attach split ring with gimp and ring hitch. Slide down the first *3* beads, then knot. Slide down the next *3* beads, knot again and continue the entire length. The knots appear between each pair of tiger's-eye beads only, holding the larger-holed bone and mother-of-pearl beads in place. When finishing off the necklace it may be necessary to extricate one of the pairs of doubled threads to facilitate the putting on of gimp in the way described on page 42, and the larger hole of the mother-of-pearl bead in the end group of 3 beads may be a useful place to conceal an extra knot, or the cut-off ends.

EARRINGS

Using the heart-shaped pendants of fancy tiger's-eye at the bottom of each earring: attach the pendant with a triangular wire bail to the bottom loop of an eyepin wire. Thread on 1 large carved bone bead, 1 large tiger's-eye, and 1 mother-of-pearl. Bend a loop at the top and attach to earring fittings in the usual way.

Project 3 Two-strand black bracelet of antique French jet pieces and embroidery beads on tigertail, with festooned earrings to match, and two similar bracelets
Project 6 Three knotted necklaces *(from below)*: lapis lazuli and crystal; fresh-water pearls and lace agate; tiger's eye, carved bone and mother-of-pearl, with earrings to match. Also shown are two pairs of cufflinks, and earrings with agate drops and silver chain

7
PENDANT NECKLACE
and Matching Earrings

This beautiful and elaborate pendant necklace of many strands uses a rose-quartz pendant and beads, antique decorated Venetian beads and embroidery beads of various types, with a tassel at the back. There are matching bead tassel earrings. The necklace length, excluding tassel and pendant, is 86cm (34in).

Materials
Creamy pink 40 nylon thread
Rose-quartz pendant
8 round and 2 cylindrical rose quartz beads
9 Venetian rosebud-decorated feature beads
Embroidery beads in pink, clear, and pale creamy-yellow, to harmonise with the colours of the main beads
Slightly larger embroidery beads 3mm (1/8in), honey colour, with slightly larger holes

There are 4 separate parallel strands running the length of the necklace, knotted together regularly and all going through the special beads, with their ends forming the tassel at the back of the neck. Two strands are threaded with the pink embroidery beads, 1 with clear and 1 with yellow.

1st strand
Double thread 183cm (72in), start with temporary knot.
1 pink embroidery bead, 1 larger honey, 5cm (2in) of pink embroidery beads,
1 honey, 4cm (1½in) pink embroidery beads. (This end will form part of the tassel.) Then:
1 honey, 1st rose quartz, 1 honey, 4cm (1½in) embroidery beads,
1 honey, 1st Venetian, 1 honey, 4cm (1½in) embroidery beads,
1 honey, 2nd rose quartz, 1 honey, 4cm (1½in) embroidery beads,
1 honey, 2nd Venetian, 1 honey, 4cm (1½in) embroidery beads,
1 honey, 1st rose quartz cylinder, 1 honey, 4cm (1½in) embroidery beads,
1 honey, 3rd Venetian, 1 honey, 4cm (1½in) embroidery beads,

1 honey, 3rd rose quartz, 1 honey, 4cm (1½in) embroidery beads.
    At the centre: 1 honey, 4th Venetian, 1 honey, 1cm (²/5in) pink embroidery beads, through pendant, 1cm (³/8in) pink embroidery beads, back through last honey, Venetian and honey,
* 4cm (1½in) embroidery beads, 1 honey, 4th rose quartz, 1 honey,
4cm (1½in) embroidery beads, 1 honey, 5th Venetian, 1 honey,
4cm (1½in) embroidery beads, 1 honey, 2nd rose quartz cylinder, 1 honey,
4cm (1½in) embroidery beads, 1 honey, 6th Venetian, 1 honey,
4cm (1½in) embroidery beads, 1 honey, 5th rose quartz, 1 honey,
4cm (1½in) embroidery beads, 1 honey, 7th Venetian, 1 honey,
4cm (1½in) embroidery beads, 1 honey, 6th rose quartz, 1 honey,
4cm (1½in) embroidery beads, 1 honey.
    Then, for tassel: 5cm (2in) embroidery beads, 1 honey, 1 pink embroidery bead, finish with a temporary knot, and leave fairly loose.

Second and third strands
These are almost exactly the same as the first strand. One uses the same pink embroidery beads, the other uses the clear glass embroidery beads instead of the pink. The second and third threads go through all the same honey, rose quartz and Venetian beads as the first strand, but separate to thread on the small embroidery beads. At the centre: the second and third threads do not go through the pendant.

Fourth strand
The fourth strand will also go through all the same honey, rose quartz and Venetian beads as the first three. Start and finish with a length of 5cm (2in) yellow embroidery beads for the tassel, but thereafter thread a sequence of only 32mm (1¼in) between each large bead and do not go through the pendant. When finally knotted, this will allow each group of strands to bunch out attractively.

a

b

c

Knotting a multistrand pendant necklace with rose quartz, Venetian and embroidery beads. With the pendant at the centre of the thread, tie one overhand knot above the loop of embroidery beads but below the honey bead, and another above the honey bead on top of the Venetian bead, but below the main necklace (a). Remove the sellotape which is preventing the beads sliding together and make an overhand knot with the four strands together on the left side of the necklace (b). Slide the first sequence of embroidery beads down towards the centre and follow the rest of the sequence above. Once you have completed the left-hand side do the same with the right (c)

Knotting

Slide the pendant as near as possible to the centre of the thread and make an overhand knot above the little loop of embroidery beads and underneath the honey bead, with the double strands that go through the pendant loop as shown in the illustration. Make another knot above the honey bead on top of the Venetian bead. Now remove your bits of sellotape. Carefully, and starting with the left hand side of the necklace, make an overhand knot with the 4 strands of the left-hand bunch together, *as if* they had all emerged from the pendant etc. Now push that first bunch of embroidery beads down their strands and tie an overhand knot leaving no exposed thread.

Slide down the honey, rose quartz and honey beads, tie another overhand knot, slide down the next bunch of embroidery beads, tie overhand knot, slide down honey, Venetian, honey, tie overhand knot, next bunch embroidery beads, overhand knot, honey, rose quartz cylinder, honey, overhand knot, next bunch embroidery beads, overhand knot, honey, Venetian, honey, overhand knot, next bunch embroidery beads, overhand knot, honey, rose quartz bead, honey, overhand knot, next bunch embroidery beads, overhand knot, honey, Venetian, honey, overhand knot, next bunch embroidery beads, overhand knot, honey, rose quartz bead, honey, overhand knot, next bunch embroidery beads, and wait before creating the tassel with the final bunches at the end. Do the same up the other side, making sure there is as little slack as possible (the different lengths of embroidery beads allow a loopy bunched effect). Now take the strands of both sides together and tie an overhand knot, with another next to it. This allows the tassel to hang nicely. Undo your 8 temporary knots one at a time, push up the beads and finish each tassel strand with an overhand knot, singed to a neat blob.

EARRINGS

These earrings with tassels are each made of 4 strands of thread with embroidery beads, making an 8 stranded tassel. Though not simple to make, the results are really grand.

Start with a thread about 51cm (20in) long. As on the necklace, start each strand with a temporary knot, then thread 1 pink, 1 honey, 40mm (1½in) embroidery beads, 1 honey bead, 1 Venetian, 1 honey, rose quartz, honey, 10mm (²⁄₅in) embroidery beads, through the loop of the earring clasp, another 10mm (²⁄₅in) embroidery beads, back through the honey, rose quartz and Venetian beads, then a *new* honey bead, 40mm (1½in) embroidery beads, honey, pink embroidery bead and another temporary knot.

Next strand: temporary knot, pink, honey, 40mm (1½in) embroidery beads, through 1 of the honey beads already threaded. Up through Venetian bead and honey, rose quartz and honey at top. Make a half-hitch around the base of the loop before returning through the honey, rose quartz, honey, Venetian, sequence. Then through another new honey, 40mm (1½in) embroidery beads, honey and pink, temporary knot. Thread another 2 strands similarly, but go up and down through the honey beads already there to result in 3 honeys below the Venetian bead, 2 with 3 strands and 1 with 2 emerging. Now loosen away from the top loop, make an overhand knot with all the strands just below the rose quartz, then slide up the strands and finish with overhand knots singed at each of the ends to form the tassel.

Project 7 Beautiful and elaborate long necklace with rose quartz pendant and beads, antique Venetian rosebud decorated beads, and various embroidery beads; with tassel earrings to match

GLOSSARY

This is a list of specific terms associated with beads and beadwork, including common or descriptive names of bead types, materials, tools, findings and processes involved, and places and peoples particularly strongly associated with bead manufacture, trade or use. Derivations of names and terms are not generally included, being the subject of future research.

Some of the bead names are either traditional (cube allies), or manufacturers' names (dofa or cut tosca), many of which are becoming obsolete as manufacturers and importers go metric, streamline their bookkeeping and discontinue less fashionable lines. Some names have already come adrift from their meanings, such as Wynberg beads, available, according to a pattern leaflet, for jewellery making in 1913; or OP beads, in common use in the last century and known to be large cylindrical glass beads, but what OP signifies seems to have been forgotten. (Any known name associated with a particular bead has been included, and the author would be pleased to learn anything further.)

Apart from the obvious shape names understood by everyone such as round or oblong, I have only included the proper names of typical bead shapes that occur frequently (oblate, bicone, cornerless cube, etc.) and which are less immediately understood by a novice. For further reference the student is recommended to consult Horace Beck's *Classification and Nomenclature of Beads and Pendants* and *A Dictionary of Bead Terms* by Peter Francis (see Bibliography). Similarly, though common gemstone names are included, there are several good books offering detailed information.

ABALONE Iridescent multicoloured blue-grey shell cut or carved into beads, pendants and inlays (paui shell in New Zealand)

ABO BEAD Cylinder or disc bead of reddish bauxite, from Nigeria, not to be confused with coral

ADJÁGBA Type of powder glass bead from Ghana, rounded and oval shapes, plain colours, stripes

AFRICAN TRADE BEADS Decorated hand-made glass beads were brought into Africa from the seventeenth century on by every trader, most of which were made in Venice but could be described as African by use. Old stone and glass beads were also brought by Arab traders from India, and some even older Roman glass beads may have found their way along the trade routes.

AFRO BEADED HAIRSTYLE *See* HAIR BEAD

AGATE Semi-precious, variegated, layered, translucent stone in a range of colours, can be dyed. Has been carved into beads etc. since most ancient times.

AGATE WARE Ceramic technique of creating an integral pattern using different coloured clays rolled or pressed together, not just on the surface. Attractive porcelain beads can be hand made this way.

Front section of a choker constructed of old Tibetan agate beads, with garnet pebbles, Ethiopian silver, and brown embroidery beads

AGGREY Very old traditional name in Ghana, Nigeria, etc. for ornate trail decorated glass beads made for African trade.

AKOSU Old decorated sandcast powder glass from Ghana, often 'eye' or loop patterns

ALABASTER 1 also known as onyx marble, one of the softer stones, milky-translucent or opaque, creamy-white, yellowy, green, brown, easily carved and stained, and used to make beads in Pakistan and Mexico 2 Milky glass beads intended for coating with a layer of pearl varnish as imitation pearls

ALMANDINE Popular deep purplish-red gemstone, garnet family

ALPHABET BEAD Moulded opaque glass bead with letter, so a necklace can be a message or a name tag

ALUMINIUM Beads and pendants are made in Kenya by the Turkana, using recycled saucepans

AMAZONITE Opaque mottled or grainy-looking light green semi-precious stone

AMBASSADOR BEAD Old blue hexagonal prism-shaped cylindrical European glass trade bead, appears in Zimbabwe

AMBER From 50 million years BC. Fossilised pine tree resin, extremely light, opaque or transparent mustard, gold, honey-brown shades. Revered and valued as a gemstone, earliest beads from the Baltic. Confused

with copal resin, ambroid, horn and plastics.

AMBROID Victorian process for reconstituting lumps of amber from tiny chippings. Less brittle than natural amber. Texture looks like cirrus clouds.

AMERICAN INDIAN BEADWORK Particularly understood in Britain as beadweaving, but, as in Africa, they used beads with every possible threading and embroidery technique

AMETHYST Mauve to purple member of quartz family, semi-precious

AMSTERDAM Dutch glass-bead industry centred in Amsterdam, started to produce trade beads in the seventeenth century, similar to Venetian types such as 'chevron'. Still very difficult to discern and establish the differences.

AMULET Often a pendant or jewellery component worn for its protective magical power

ANCIENT BEADS Vague term normally describing beads of Roman period or earlier

ANKH Motif of cross with wide loop at the top, a popular ancient Egyptian symbol of life, rebirth, resurrection, often worn as a pendant or talisman or incorporated into jewellery designs

ANKLET Ankle bracelet

ANNULAR Ring shaped

ANODISING Method of colouring aluminium used in modern costume jewellery

ANTIQUE Over one hundred years old (otherwise 'collectable')

APACHE BEADWORK See American Indian beadwork

APATITE Semi-precious clear stone, pink, yellow, green, violet or cat's eye type. Softer than tourmaline with which it can be confused.

APPLE CORAL A porous coral formation from Philippines impregnated with tinted resin to make attractive beads

AQUAMARINE Transparent watery-blue precious gemstone

ARAGONITE Also known as onyx marble, oriental alabaster

ARMLET, ARMBAND Bracelet for the upper arm

ARROWHEAD Common shape of pendant, strung on its own or often component of ancient or 'primitive' type necklaces

ART DECO Necklaces of the art deco period (between the two world wars) with the characteristic strong angular geometric shapes or bold colours predominating, using moulded and faceted Czech glass beads or involving early and positive use of plastics (casein, Bakelite, celluloid, etc.) and chrome, not intended to imitate but exploiting their own decorative potential. Also industrial, Egyptian or 'grotesque' motifs.

ART NOUVEAU Late Victorian, Edwardian period;

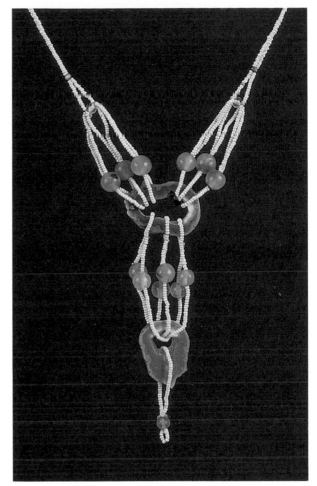

Necklace constructed or polished agate geode slices and beads, and cream pearl embroidery beads

Lalique and Tiffany were exponents of the fluid line, organic and stylised natural forms and colours, a style vigorously expressed in jewellery, sometimes using beads, but not any particular type of bead

ARTIFICIAL PEARLS Man-made beads resembling pearls. Hollow glass bubble beads coated on the inside with a pearl varnish, or plain 'alabaster' glass beads coated on the outside.

ARTS AND CRAFTS MOVEMENT Mid-nineteenth century onwards, led by William Morris. Reacting to the impersonal trend of industrial production, while not condemning it, a renewed evaluation of the simple direct craft processes of the designer/ craftsperson in every discipline. Jewellery produced included silver, pewter, hand-made chainlinks with beads and pendants, which can often look 'folksy' or 'medieval'.

ASHANTI Tribes in Ghana and Nigeria, famous for making gold and bronze pendants and jewellery by 'lost wax' casting methods, also beads made of ground up European glass fused in clay moulds

AURORA BOREALIS Manufacturer's name for faceted crystal glass beads with added iridescent coating. Very expensive, characteristic beads from Swarovsky in Austria.

AUSTRIA Bohemian glass industry refugees set up factories in Austria

AVENTURINE 1 Aventurine glass or goldstone. 2 Semi-precious gemstone, generally green, quartz family, with tiny visible glittery specks. Incorrectly known as Indian jade, sometimes deep blue or brownish in colour.

AXHEAD Trapezium-shaped pendant, drilled through the narrowest edge

BAIL Wire triangle to attach a pendant to a loop or chain

BAKELITE An early plastic, invented 1909, used to manufacture many items including moulded beads and jewellery components

BALTIC COAST See amber

BALUSTRADE BEAD Large glass balustrade-shaped bead on the Chinese 'Mandarin' beads next to tassel

BAMBOO Hollow stalks of bamboo, almost indestructible, an ideal material to make cylindrical beads in quantity (for example bead curtains)

BANDEAU Flexible hair band, could be beadwork

BANDED AGATE Some of the most decorative forms of agate have different coloured strata or layers which can be artificially stained to accentuate the contrasting bands. When black and white often confusingly called onyx. In the Himalayas natural banded agates are particularly prized. Skill in cutting is needed to display banding to maximum effect.

BANGLE Rigid ring-shaped bracelet sometimes decorated with added tiny beads

BARBARIC Type of swirled glass bead required for a 1913 pattern

BAROQUE Any irregular rounded stone, glass or pearl bead

BARREL Common name for shape of bead, or of screw fastener

BATIK Decoration technique using wax-resist and dye which works well on unvarnished wood beads

BAUBLE Any decorative dangling trinket

BAUXITE Soft reddish aluminium ore made into abo beads, discs or cylinders in Nigeria. Not to be confused with coral, for which it may be used as a substitute.

BEAD From Anglo-Saxon *bidden*, to pray, tell one's beads. Any small or rounded component with a hole through it, to be strung, singly or with others in a sequence.

BEAD CUP Cup- or flowerpot-shaped component with central hole which combines with beads of other shapes in designs or may conceal a knot where several bead strands are gathered together

BEAD EMBROIDERY Technique of embellishing textiles and garments with stitched-on beads

BEAD LOOM Framework for stretching warp threads for beadweaving, specially constructed with rollers to accommodate extended length; or threads may be wound round a stout cardboard box or a springy strip of wood or laminate and used as a bow loom

BEADING NEEDLE Extremely fine needle sizes 10–16 used only for bead lace, bead embroidery and bead-weaving

BEADING TIP Type of finding for attaching thread to clasp. Knot sits inside a small concave shape attached to a bent metal loop.

BEADWEAVING Style of patterned beaded textile construction developed by, or associated with, North American Indians. Also a nineteenth-century technique in Europe and USA for decorative bands for jewellery and many ornamental knick-knacks, little purses, etc. which can be made of strips stitched together.

BEADWORK General term for techniques using embroidery beads: bead lace, beadweaving, bead embroidery, tambour beading, bead knitting, bead crochet, etc.

BEANS Often pierced and used as beads, many colourful varieties. Very large shiny brown ones worn as protective amulets by expectant mothers in Kenya.

BEECH Wood ideal for mass production of wood beads, plain colours or varnished

BEESWAX Used to strengthen and stiffen thread

BEETLE Iridescent green beetles' bodies used as jewellery components mounted, or used threaded as beads (*see also* scarab)

BEGGAR BEADS cheap strings of multicoloured alternating long and round or cornerless cube beads of agate and jasper, with fat Turk's head knots or small metal beads in between, from India

BELL Small metal bells incorporated with beads and as pendants, especially in 'hippy' era when their tinkling was an added attraction

BELL CAP Finding to convert undrilled stone into a pendant by gluing

BELT Many forms of beadwork are used to construct and decorate belts, and also girdles

BENIN In West Africa, outstanding ivory carving, and traditional and elaborate royal regalia constructed with great numbers of huge coral beads

BERYL Precious gemstone usually transparent gold or yellow

BICONE Typical bead shape, tapering to a cone at both ends

BIDA In Nigeria, a centre of bead trading and a small glass bead-making industry, recycling glass beer bottles, etc.

BIRDCAGE BEAD Some large clear beads on lace bobbins are embellished with added rows of tiny beads on wire

BIRMINGHAM BEAD Venetian trade bead in Africa, round, white with blue dots

BIRTHSTONE Gemstones belonging to zodiac signs or months, worn for good luck or as a protective talisman

BLOOD KNOT Knot for tying stiff gut

BLOODSTONE *See* jasper

BLOWN-GLASS BEAD Bead made by shaping a tube of molten glass into hollow bubbles with two holes by blowing freely or into mould

BOBBIN SPANGLE BEADS Distinctive hand-made glass beads possibly made in England to decorate English lace bobbins. Of lampwork with marvering, crumb, or squiggle decoration.

BODOM Mysterious large ancient fused glass bead, generally with a black centre, yellow surface and coloured decoration, found in Ghana and possibly made there

BOG OAK A black wood carved into beads from Ireland. Can be confused with jet or ebony, but coarser.

BOHEMIA In the district of Gablonz (now Jablonec in Czechoslovakia) a glass industry was established by runaway Venetians, which became second in importance in world glass-bead production, especially moulded glass shapes.

BOLO Plaited thong bootlace tie

BOLT RING Common necklace fastening

BONE Camel, monkey or other bone, carved and used as an alternative to ivory, its texture having a coarser, more splintery, 'grain'

BOSUN'S WHISTLE Knot with possible uses in bead threading

BOTTLE GLASS Coloured medicine and beer bottles used as raw materials to recycle as fused glass beads, in West Africa

BOTTOM BEAD The largest centre bead on an English lace bobbin spangle

BOW A most versatile temporary fastening knot and decorative element using tape, ribbon, etc.

BOW DRILL Primitive but effective drill mechanism; many ancient stone beads were drilled with a bow drill (in illustrations of beadmaking from ancient Egypt)

BOWENITE Soft carvable stone resembling jade in yellow-green to brown

BOX SNAP A secure type of fastener, one half pushes in and snaps into place inside container-shaped other half, and to open, a springy lever is pressed down

BOXWOOD A fine-grained wood excellent for very detailed carving, such as elaborate rosary beads

BRACELET Jewellery worn at the wrist often of threaded beads

BRACTEATE Metal plate threaded singly or more, and used as a pendant

BRAIDING Fibres or yarns may be plaited or braided to make a thicker firmer cord for threading

BRASS A yellow metal alloy (copper and zinc), versatile as beads, it can be cast, milled, turned, hammered, engraved, stamped, pierced, soldered, etc.

BRAZIL Country or origin of many of the best gemstones, including beads

BRISINGAMEN The legendary necklace of the Norse goddess Freya

BRISTOL GLASS A particular transparent deep-blue glass, not exclusive to beads

BROACHER Tool for scraping and clearing out the holes inside beads

BRONZE A metal alloy; beads of bronze are made by casting in moulds, West Africa

BROOCH Ornamental pin to fasten or decorate clothing. Beads sometimes arranged in threaded bunches or clusters on brooches to sparkle when the wearer moves.

BUDDHIST PRAYER BEADS A string of 108 beads, sometimes with extra strings and dangling pendants at intervals, Chinese Mandarin beads being one version

BUGLE Smallest tubular glass embroidery bead

BULLA Flat or rounded metal pendant or charm case, common in Roman jewellery

BULLION Finest silver or gold or plated tubular wire coil to protect thread through fastener loops (sometimes misspelt bouillon), also known as gimp, purl, necklet ends and French wire

BUTTERFLY KNOT Decorative knot often combined with beads in Chinese necklaces, pendants, tassels, etc.

BUTTON Knob or disc with holes or a shank for stitching. Although decorative, buttons, unlike beads, have always been primarily functional but they are used in threaded jewellery, embroidery and appliqué.

CAIRNGORM Smoky quartz, grey to brown variety of transparent quartz, from Scotland but many other locations too

CALLOTTE Base metal finding for attaching knotted ends of necklace threads to fastener loops without exposed knots

CAMBAY West coast of India, ancient trade centre and port. Semi-precious stone beads may have been fashioned here and were certainly exported west towards Arabia and Africa from the fourteenth century, maybe earlier.

CANE A long rod of drawn-out coloured glass as a raw material, ready to melt the end and used to construct and decorate wound beads. Also, very elaborate canes with patterned cross-section may be made, cut in slices and fused to the side of a glass bead. *See also* chequerboard, face bead, millefiori.

CANTON *See* China

CANVAS WORK Victorian bead embroidery on canvas backing, as seen on footstools, tea-cosies, fire-screens, clock stands, trays, belts, slippers, etc. Any cross stitch or needlepoint pattern of appropriate scale will adapt for beads.

CARBUNCLE Another name for garnet

CARNELIAN Alternative spelling of cornelian, q.v.

CARVING To create or decorate a form by cutting, whittling, scraping, hollowing, etc.

CASEIN A plastic made of solid milk protein, also called galalith

CASTING To create a form using molten glass, plastic or metal, etc. in a mould. One of the commonest methods of mass production, of glass beads in particular.

CATCH Any type of fastener

CELLULOID Trade name of an early plastic, mid-nineteenth century, used to make beads

CELTS 600BC onwards, Britain and neighbouring Europe, a race which produced, used and traded glass beads before and during Roman period

CERAMIC Every kind of fired pottery, including faience, terracotta, earthenware, stoneware, porcelain, raku. Beads are and have been made of every type.

CHAIN Line of continuously linked metal loops used like thread, or to connect elements including beads, or to carry a single pendant; or the word is used generally to mean necklace

CHALCEDONY Generic term for a large group of semi-precious stones: quartz, agate, cornelian, jasper, etc.

CHALK Opaque white glass beads

CHAPLET A string of beads for the head, or a small rosary

CHARLOTTE Type of embroidery beads faceted on the outside; old trade term

CHARM Object with magical, talismanic or amuletic properties, often a bead or pendant

CHARM CASE Hollow pendant to contain a charm, or fragment of scripture, or bead of characteristic shape, which often appears in Islamic jewellery: cylindrical with loops or lugs on top edge.

CHENIER Fine metal tubing

CHEQUERBOARD Ornate millefiori-type patterned beads with squared patterns, made by ancient Chinese, Romans, Vikings and Venetians

CHEVRON Particularly valued form of trade bead, originally Venetian, later copied by Dutch. Glass tube formed as a hollow millefiori cane with star pattern cross-section of many layers, most usually red, white and blue, blue on the outside. Conical ground-down ends display the pattern as a zig-zag (like a sharpened pencil). Also called paternoster, rosetta, bakim-mutum, star bead.

CHINA 1 Country of manufacture of various types of beads including glass since 1st millennium BC. Canton or Peking glass beads made in significant quantities since mid-seventeenth century.

2 Opaque glass beads of any colour

CHIP Irregular semi-precious stone fragment drilled and polished, also known as baroque

CHOKER Very close-fitting short necklace, can be multistrand (pearls) with spacers, as a broad upright snug-fitting collar

CHRYSOCOLLA Vivid green-blue swirly opaque stone, Eilat stone being one variety

CHRYSOPRASE Paleish green almost opaque stone, quartz family

CINNABAR Vermilion red pigment of mineral origin, used on Chinese red lacquered beads

CIRE PERDUE *See* lost wax

CITRINE Yellow or brown transparent quartz

CLASP Fastener

CLAY Raw material of ceramic products

COIL Short cylindrical wire coils can be used as beads, or flat coils as pendants, as in Kenya, where the raw material is brass telephone wire

COINS Sometimes drilled and strung as pendants as visible wealth, dowry, etc., and also used as a source of fine metal, as in Ethiopia, where Portuguese silver coins were melted and made into beads and small pendants

COLLAR Beadwork collars of either a strip making a straight choker, or spread out in a circular honeycomb pattern (Zulu, etc.)

COLLARED BEAD Rounded metal bead form with small wall around the hole at each end; typical traditional Indian bead form

Ceramic beads.
Outside: 'agateware' pierced and threaded discs, with the words 'Protean' and 'Dunster' on their backs. Modern hand-made marbled porcelain. Loose Chinese porcelain beads including pink hollow porcelain 'lace' beads.
Centre: Maiolica beads from Gubbio and Deruta in Italy, with pious Latin mottoes and original linen tassel in centre

COMBED DECORATION Swirled pattern made on lampwork glass bead by dragging a pointed tool through still molten multicoloured surface

CONE One of the basic bead shapes

CONGO BEAD Moulded large-holed plain bead, suitable for thong, hair, etc.

CONNEMARA MARBLE A pale green serpentine from Ireland, made into souvenirs including beads

CONTERIE Italian, beads for counting or telling, now used as a general term for glass beads

COPAL AMBER Resembling amber; also a fossilised natural resin, or a soft natural resin that can be formed and hardened for use as a substitute for real amber. Copal beads are often very large, used in many areas of Africa.

COPPER Hammered into beads in Kenya

CORAL The twig-like framework of colonies of sea organisms which takes years to form; precious coral is an orange red to palest pink or white, fished out of the Mediterranean in particular, now becoming scarce. Golden coral, black coral, sponge coral, apple coral, fossil coral, etc. are related, and also in danger from overfishing and becoming extinct.

CORALLINE Imitation coral

CORD Three or more yarns twisted together

CORK Can be used for beads, with the advantage of lightness

CORNALINE D'ALEPPO Name of a particular Venetian trade bead with a transparent rose-coloured layer outside, another colour core, usually white or yellow. The beads are round or cylindrical, also called white hearts.

CORNELIAN Handsome red-brown variety of agate, widely used to make beads

CORNERLESS CUBE Typical bead shape of cut, faceted stones through the ages

COTTON Threading fibre in use in India, but not very strong

COTTON-WOOL BEAD Beads of compressed cotton wool used for hobbies such as toy-making, haberdashery, lampshade trimmings, with varied applications; can be embroidered

COUNTERPOISE, COUNTERWEIGHT For a heavy necklace, collar or pendant, the weight is offset with another pendant at the back, as seen in ancient Egyptian and Chinese Mandarin regalia

COWRIE SHELL Used decoratively as beads and as currency since earliest times, apparently shipped to Africa from the Maldives

CRAMPING BEAD, CRIMPING BEAD, CRIMP Very small soft metal beads used with stiff threading materials that don't knot which secure the loops connecting with fasteners at each end by being squeezed tight to grip the loop permanently shut.

CRISTALLAI One of the Venetian glass beadmakers' guilds

CROCHET A beaded fabric can be made by crochet, using yarn with all the beads already threaded on. The hook does not go through the beads.

CROW BEAD A Congo bead (q.v.) from a North American Indian tribe from Montana

CRUMB DECORATION Crumbs of coloured glass melted onto surface, can be knobbly or smooth

CRYSTAL 1 Natural clear quartz, gemstone, usually cut with facets as beads
2 Very clear and sparkly faceted cut-glass beads resembling the gemstone, expensive

CUBE ALLY Popular traditional name for moulded cylindrical or tile bead

CUT GARNET Name in old catalogues and patterns for fine strong linen thread, and originally the tiny embroidery beads threaded on it

CUT STEEL Tiny glittery embroidery beads of faceted steel

CUT TOSCA Faceted embroidery beads with square hole; old trade name

CZECHOSLOVAKIA Formerly Bohemia (until 1918), was and still is one of the major bead-producing countries. Glass industry centres on the city of Jablonec (Gablonz).

DACRON A strong modern synthetic fibre, can be used for stringing

DALLY Long necklace possibly with pendant intended to dangle seductively between the breasts

DENTALIUM SHELL Long hollow slightly curved white or greyish conical sea shell which threads easily

DIADEM Jewelled headband or head ornament denoting rank

DIAMANTÉ Any faceted glittery glass 'jewel' or bead as style of decoration, known as rhinestone in USA

DIAMOND 1 The most precious and hardest gemstone, not drilled as beads. Its hardness makes it useful for drilling and grinding facets on other stones.
2 The faceted diamond shape often occurs in beads, sometimes called lozenge

DICE Cube-shaped bead, often drilled corner to corner

DISC Very common bead shape which fits usefully between large or round beads as a spacer, or threaded together makes a smooth flexible cylinder (see heishi).

DOFA Manufacturer's name for iridescent finish on faceted black glass

DOG COLLAR Narrow tight-fitting choker necklace formed like a strip upright around the throat

DOGON Tribe in Mali, Africa, who make beautiful

mottled granite beads

DONKEY BEAD Large bead made in Qom, Iran, of turquoise faience worn by donkeys for magical protection

DORJE Metal Tibetan thunderbolt shape, included in Tibetan Buddhist prayer beads

DOUBLE BEADS Lampwork beads made in quantity in India amongst other places. Occasionally they come still joined together and can be used as such. Also known as segmented beads.

DOUGHNUT BEAD Ring-shaped glass

DRAGGED Molten glass patterns can be varied by dragging across the surface with a tool, like stirring syrup on hot porridge

DRAWN GLASS TUBE or CANE Plain or patterned canes or tubes of glass are made fat then drawn out long and thin for use as beads. Many variations.

DRILL Versatile electric motor drills with hard metal- or diamond-tipped drill bits can pierce almost any stone, metal, pearl, shell, wood or plastic. Laser drills have also been developed commercially.

DROP Common bead or pendant shape

DUSTED Sprinkled powdered glass coating on lampwork

DUTCH See Amsterdam

DYEING Any porous material (wood, pottery, shell, pearl, coral, ivory, horn and bone, as well as alabaster, soapstone, plastic and artificial pearls) can be stained with cold water dyes

DZI (or TZI) BEAD Extremely old and valued in Tibet and Himalayas, etched agate bead, large torpedo-shaped agate artificially darkened and lightened to create design of white lines, circles, waves etc. Exact age and origin unknown, imitated this century in lampwork glass and early plastic.

EARCLIP Ornament attached flat to ear lobe, sometimes with dangling beads or drops

EARTHENWARE See ceramic

EBONY Brown-black fine-grained wood, often used for turned and carved beads

EGYPTIAN PASTE A fine special formula clay which includes its own colour and glaze so one firing is sufficient. Similar recipe used for ancient Egyptian bead production, for example in Tel el Amarna. Turquoise blue is the commonest colour but also green, deep blue, black, purple, brown, earth red and ochre yellow.

EILAT STONE See chrysocolla

ELASTIC Round shirring or hat elastic can be used for threading bracelets and necklaces, the advantage being that it needs no clasp as it will stretch to go on and off

ELECTRUM Natural alloy of silver and gold

ELEPHANT IVORY True ivory is the tusks of the elephant. Modern use is discouraged as elephants are endangered.

ELEPHANT SHAPE A very popular animal frequently depicted on Indian jewellery including pendants and beads

EMBROIDERY BEAD See bugle, rocaille

EMERALD Precious stone drilled and used as beads in Indian jewellery, Moghul style

ENAMELLING A way of decorating metal beads with colour and pattern. True enamel is a vitreous substance that has to be melted into place in a kiln, and can be transparent or opaque. Enamelling is found on beads from Byzantine Europe. Traditional Chinese beads and pendants are often decorated with cloisonné enamel – decorative wire outlines embedded in the enamel, also used by some designer craftsmen of today.

'END OF DAY GLASS' BEAD Moulded bead which appears to be made using up mixed coloured-glass leftovers

ENGRAVING Method of embellishing metal by incised line patterns

ETCH Method of adding pattern to metal by use of acid to eat into surface

ETHIOPIA Typical from Ethiopia are small tubular and larger round silver beads and Coptic cross pendants

ETHNIC Term which has come to mean anything primitive, folksy, low technology or Third World. Ethnic beads may in fact include glass trade beads originally made in Europe.

ETRURIA The Etruscans used incredibly fine and exact gold granulation techniques, including for beads, subsequently lost for centuries, now being redeveloped

EYE BEAD A large category of types of decorated glass beads from most ancient to present day, which can be millefiori, trailed, raised or smooth, with many eyes or one. Used as a protective amulet to ward off the gaze of the evil eye.

EYEPIN Wire finding with loop already formed at one end for holding beads, either as a link in a chain or to dangle from an earring fitting

FACE BEAD Glass, faience, trail decorated, moulded or with millefiori with face design. Ancient beads to present day have used this motif, not surprisingly, and old specimens are rare, expensive and very collectable.

FACETED Moulded or wound glass with flattened or cut, ground or polished reflective surfaces or facets, normally transparent glass

FAIENCE *See* ceramic, Egyptian paste

FANCY OR PHANTASY Trail decorations on lampwork glass beads

FEATHERING A particular combed or dragged pattern on lampwork glass beads

FELDSPAR Group of semi-precious gemstones including amazonite, moonstone and the beautiful labradorite

FERRONIÈRE Chain with jewel at front, worn on lady's head

FERRULE Some clasps are attached by the chain or thread end being secured with solder, glue or a concealed knot inside a small length of metal tubing

FETISH Amulet, pendant or charm, often representing a person, animal or thing

FIGURE OF EIGHT KNOT Knot with bead-threading applications

FILE Useful as tool for smoothing down metal, shell, wood or the softest of stones

FILIGREE Goldsmithing technique producing fine intricate patterned structures with plain and twisted wires, used in many ways to make exquisite decorative metal beads, also clasps

FILLET Another word for headband

FINDINGS Term denoting all types of metal fastenings and jewellery construction components which can be purchased ready made

FISHING LINE Nylon monofilament gut

FLINT Earliest cutting tools were made of flint, including, probably, sharp fragments set on the point of a drill

FLOSS Dental floss is extremely strong fine unspun thread, and can be used for bead threading if waxed

FLUORSPAR Transparent semi-precious gemstone, comes in many colours, the best known being blue john found in Derbyshire

FLUTING Cut in, grooved, longitudinal decoration on beads

FOIL Fine silver, or rarely gold leaf or foil incorporated inside layers of transparent glass to increase reflective quality and intensify the colour. Some Roman glass beads had gold foil. The technique was rediscovered in the nineteenth and twentieth centuries in Venetian, Czech and Japanese bead making.

FOLDED GLASS Ancient process of making beads by folding a flat blob of glass around a mandrel

FOSSIL Some of the earliest known beads to survive are made of fossil crinoid sections with holes artificially enlarged

FOSSIL CORAL A decorative brown stone covered with coral patterns from, amongst other places, Arizona

FOXTAIL Very fine smooth slinky chain preferred to other types of chain for threading beads

FRENCH JET Name for any faceted black glass bead that resembles jet, not necessarily antique

FRINGE Beaded fringes embellish lampshades and other furnishings, as well as jewellery, garments and hair accessories, where they dangle and shimmer

FRIT *See* Egyptian paste

FROSTING Slightly roughened surface on clear or coloured glass; lessens transparency

FUMED Surface on glass beads with iridescent effect achieved by fuming

GADROONED Fluted

GALONS Braided or lace trimmings, may incorporate small beads

GARLAND Floral headband or necklace

GARNET Dark red, semi-precious stone often made into small beads

GASHI *See* powder glass

GEMSTONE Any form of admired and valued mineral stone both precious and semi-precious, generally embracing jet, amber, coral, pearls and even ivory. Can be left natural but rendered more valuable by shaping, cutting facets, drilling, threading or setting.

GESSO A modelling compound mainly of plaster and glue, dries quite tough and can be painted, gilded, varnished etc.

GILDING METAL or TOMBAC Non-ferrous alloy intended to take gold plating

GILT Gold plating, surface coating of very thin layer of gold

GIMP *See* bullion

GIRDLE A loose decorative belt, can be of beads or beaded

GLAZE To cover with a thin layer of melted glass for decoration and protection, particularly on porous ceramic composition but also softer stone beads, such as steatite, glazed in ancient Egypt

GOLD The most versatile and valuable precious metal throughout history, associated with nobility and riches as well as beauty

GOLDFILL USA name for rolled gold, q.v.

GOLDSTONE Not a natural stone but a glittery metallic effect produced within glass or enamels with copper filings, sometimes called aventurine

GORGET Flat throat ornament at front of choker

Antique Chinese baskets decorated with coins, glass beads and tassels; also a long Chinese necklace of verdite and carved amethyst, on silver wire links

GOURD 1 Bead shape (Chinese beads)
2 African percussion musical instrument: a dried hollow gourd or calabash encased in a loose net threaded with beads that rattle when shaken
GRADUATED BEADS Single or multistrand necklace of pearls or beads of one material with the largest hanging at the centre front then getting progressively smaller up to the centre back or the clasp
GRANITE *See* Dogon
GRANULATION *See* Etruria
GRASS KNOT BEAD Made in India, Mexico and Pacific Islands
GREENLAND Name used in Holland for fancy bead-work collars that look like Fair Isle sweater decoration, and the rocaille beads used to make them
GREY LACE AGATE Attractive pale stratified agate
GRINDING Method of cutting and polishing smooth facets on stone or glass beads using abrasive grits
GROOVED BEAD 1 *See* fluting
2 Undrilled stone with groove attached by tying with thread or wire around the grooves
GULAMIN A town in Morocco. Name given to Venetian millefiori cylindrical trade beads but not their place of origin. Collected by hippies.
GUT *See* nylon monofilament gut
GYPSUM Extremely soft stone; alabaster (onyx marble) is in the gypsum family, so is steatite (soapstone)

HAEMATITE Semi-precious stone, black with shiny metallic lustre, very heavy
HAIR BEAD Wonderful beaded Afro hairstyles can be created by threading a series of large-holed beads onto many small plaits. As the whole style takes hours to create it is left in for several weeks until the plaits loosen next to the scalp. The beads dangle and move attractively. The effect can be imitated by adding beaded dangles to hair ornaments.
HAND OF FATIMA Figurative amulet pendant, often made of metal or glass
HARDNESS Hardness of stones is measured on Mohs scale, 1–10
HAUSA Nigerian tribe who traditionally buy and sell beads
HEADPIN Short wire on which to thread beads for earrings or pendants which looks like a pin
HEBRON BEAD Large plain very rough bubbly glass wound bead; blue, turquoise, brown, green and clear, with very large holes; hand made in the Holy Land
HEISHI (American Indian) Small shell or other disc beads (*see* disc), chiefly white. Heishi chokers were very popular for both men and women in the 1970s. Also called surfing beads.

HEXAGONAL SHAPE Many simple faceted beads have a hexagonal cross-section, either hexagonal cylinder beads or hexagonal barrels or bicones
HINDU PRAYER BEADS Earliest known prayer beads are Hindu; today often of rudraksha (q.v.) nuts
HINGE FASTENER On broad bracelets, an arrangement of a pin to be threaded through aligned tubes or loops. Often metal, or can be carved, for example of bone, ivory or horn.
HIPPO TOOTH A bead in West Africa resembling a large flat tooth but actually cut from arca shell
HOGAN Small metal, fluted, truncated bicone (to match liquid silver, q.v.); catalogue name
HOLLOW Some beads are hollow because of their construction or for lightness
HONEYCOMB Basic openwork bead lace-threading structure subject to infinite variation, also sometimes known as flat peyote stitch
HOOK AND EYE Form of fastening generally made of hammered wire
HORN Very versatile natural material for carving and shaping, all shades of cream, beige, brown, russet to black, translucent to opaque
HORSEHAIR Formerly used to thread tiniest corals and sea pearls
HUBBELL BEAD Czech blotched or crumb-decorated glass bead resembling turquoise, jade, etc., traded in the past by one company in particular in the USA
HYPOALLERGENIC (anti-allergic) Metal findings, earring wires in particular, that do not cause an allergic reaction, such as surgical steel

IDAR-OBERSTEIN Gemstone cutting, drilling and bead-making centre in Germany since early sixteenth century. When local agate, jasper, etc., started to diminish they began to import raw stone from Brazil in 1834.
IMAM Long beads with ornamental drop shape, traditional endings for Islamic prayer beads attached to tassel
IMPRESSED A surface pattern or texture may be given to a lampwork glass bead by marvering (q.v.) against a textured surface, or impressing with a tool while still viscous
INDIA A rich profusion of beads of every type have been made in various areas of India since earliest times.
INDIAN RED (mutisalah) Small earth-red glass beads produced and traded west into Africa, east and north into Indonesia, Burma, Thailand, etc.
INLAY Many interesting beads of natural substances have additional inlays of other substances, such as

Chinese and Japanese lacquer with shell, metal, and other precious substances or Middle East metal elements embedded in wood or horn, etc.

INRO Japanese small decorative dangling container held on to a belt with netsuke and ojime (q.v.)

INTERLOCKING BEAD See snake bead

IRIDESCENCE Rainbow lustre finish to outside of some beads. Part of kiln process or added afterwards or result of chemical decomposition on ancient glass.

IRIS Type of clear iridescent bead, manufacturer's name. See also dofa.

IRON Iron beads exist in Kenya (Turkana tribe)

ISLAMIC Some old bead types, particularly of cornelian, appear all along the Islamic trade routes, from north India, Afghanistan, Turkestan, mid East, North and Central Africa.

IVORY In addition to elephant tusk, only fossilised mammoth tusk or walrus tooth are allowed to be called ivory, but see also bone, vegetable ivory

JABLONEC See Czechoslovakia

JADE (jadeite or nephrite) Highly valued stone by Chinese and pre-Columbian civilisations in Central and South America. Very hard, translucent to opaque, various greenish colours often intricately carved into beads and pendants. New Zealand greenstone is nephrite.

JADEITE See jade

JAPALNALA Hindu prayer beads

JAPAN Glass beads already being made in Japan at the time of the Roman period in Europe. Also exquisitely individually carved netsuke and ojime beads, from the Edo period onwards (seventeenth century). Today modern glass beads are factory produced.

JASPER Very common opaque semi-precious stone in many variegated earthy colours

JET (lignite) Black shiny fossilised coal used as bead-making material made popular by Queen Victoria in mourning. The best jet comes from Whitby on the Yorkshire coast, but lesser quality imported from Spain.

JUG BEAD Popular name for the older type of large-holed wound hand-made glass beads. They abound in clear, brown and green, and are smooth on the inside. Often used on Victorian milk jug covers and bead curtains. Also milky-white, light blue and other opaque colours. Probably Chinese.

JUMP RING Finding; small wire ring, not soldered shut so it can be used to link other elements

KASHMIR BUGLE Type of cylindrical embroidery bead, alternatively spelt Cashmere

KENYA Many types of beads are made and used by tribes in Kenya, for example the Turkana, Maasai, Kikuyu and Samburu. The Maasai thread tiny beads on wire to produce magnificent colourful rigid circular collars, also earrings and head decorations.

KIKIRI Brass heishi-type beads from Kenya

KIRDI BRONZE BEADS AND PENDANTS From Cameroon, made by lost wax (q.v.) casting

KITTY FISHER'S EYES Traditional lace bobbin bead with charming dot design named after famous English eighteenth-century actress

KNITTING As with crochet, items may be knitted to include beads if these are counted and threaded onto the yarn beforehand

KNOTTING Important in necklace making. Correct knots between beads protect them from abrasion and loss as well as being ornamental.

KOMBOLOGION Greek worry beads

KORALEK Czech word for bead (from coral)

KOREA Early bead development in Korea ran parallel to and was as important as that of China and Japan

KROBO BEAD The Ghanaian Krobo tribe made fused powder glass beads, or altered glass beads that were imported, by heating etc.

LABRADORITE A blue-grey feldspar with wonderful rainbow iridescence

LACE, LACING A solid braided cord intended to hold things together and to be tied and untied

LACE BOBBINS Tools of the lacemaker. They hold a length of thread and for English lacemaking the ends are weighted and decorated by a spangle of glass beads. They are sometimes very ornamental, they sometimes have dates and inscriptions on them and may help us to identify certain hand-made glass beads.

LALIQUE Prolific designer (see art nouveau). Some of his jewellery included moulded glass beads that he designed.

LAMINATED Made of a number of thin layers cemented together

LAMPSHADE Victorian and Edwardian lampshades were often trimmed with bead fringes

LAMPWORK The most versatile technique of making glass beads by hand. A glass cane is held in the flame of a 'lamp' and wound round a mandrel and is shaped or smoothed by marvering or decorated with trails of molten colours while rotating to keep its shape. Many lampwork beads are now made of glass; the large ones have black coating inside the hole, the smaller ones have a chalky powder.

LAPIDARY The technique of cutting, shaping, polishing and faceting stones

LAPIS LAZULI Deep blue opaque stone, often with tiny metallic flecks. Used since antiquity, the best is mainly from Afghanistan.

LATHE Small beads of wood, ivory, bone and shell and the softer stones can be turned and shaped on a lathe

LATTICINO A lacy effect produced in small Venetian glass items including beads by winding around a cane of spirally twisted clear and white glass

LAVENDER JASPER Pale opaque mauve jasper

LAZY STITCH A bead embroidery stitch attaching several small beads on each short stitch

LEADER A small linking thread loop between needle and proper thread or between two lots of thread to allow beads to slide across

LEATHER Used as threading material in thin strips or thongs, or as ground for North American or African bead embroidery (belts, purses, slippers, etc.), or cut into discs or rolled into beads for threading

LEECH Beads of curved cylindrical shape

LENTICULAR Lentil shape, either disc-like with central hole, or tabular with hole from edge to edge

LEOPARD SKIN AGATE Attractive spotty or blotched agate from Botswana, darker and lighter grey, beige, brown

LETTER BEAD See alphabet bead

LIGNITE See jet

LINED BEAD Clear bugle bead with painted colour inside which may wash out

LIQUID SILVER Style of necklaces and jewellery with a somewhat south-west American Indian flavour, particularly single-strand chokers of tiny tubular silver beads interspersed with chips of turquoise, hogans, small carved fetishes, etc. threaded on a stiff springy gut

LOOM See bead loom

LOST WAX Method of casting in metal. The model is made in wax and coated with clay; the wax melts out of its hollow shape and molten metal can flow in. Used, for example, in Benin Nigeria to make bronze and gold jewellery and small items.

LOTUS POD So-called shape which appears in Egyptian jewellery but may in fact be opium poppy-head

LOVE BEADS Popular in the sixties. Long strings of tiny beads of all colours; many strings could be worn.

LOZENGE Diamond shape

LUCKY BEADS See shasha

LUNULA Crescent moon-shaped necklace

LUSTRE Iridescent or metallic effect on glass or glazed surface; integral part of bead, not applied afterwards

MAASAI Tribe in Kenya with a wonderful range of jewellery incorporating small beads on copper or iron wire. Colourful flat collars, earrings, pendants, belts, etc.

MACCA Small faceted bugles; Italian name

MACRAMÉ The craft of decorative knotting to create textiles, fringes, hangings and practical items. Beads often incorporated.

MALA String of Buddhist or Hindu prayer beads

MALACHITE Heavy soft vivid green opaque stone

MALI DISC Distinctive heavy large yellow, very old disc-shaped glass bead, probably Venetian or Dutch but traded and valued in Mali, West Africa

MANDARIN BEAD Antique Chinese glass bead of very large size. Sometimes on summit of hat as insignia of rank or included on their very long Mandarin necklaces. Occasionally they have T-shaped perforation and are used in conjunction with balustrade beads (q.v.)

MANDIA Lotus root carved into beads in Mali, West Africa

MANDREL Rod around which molten glass is coiled to form beads which are then slid off; see lampwork

MARVERING Finishing process for lampwork beads which are rolled across a smooth surface while still on mandrel

MASS Traditional quantity in which beads are sold

MATRIX Body core, or background colour

MATT Non-shiny surface, either intentional or the result of wear

MATTHEW WALKER Useful type of knot which ties evenly around a central cord with varying numbers of strands

MAURITANIA West African country with a strong interest in colourful glass beads and pendants; some imported from Europe; their own beads are made of powdered glass melted in elaborate designs

MEDALLION Large round pendant like a medal or coin, maybe commemorative or as an award or purely decorative; acceptable as male jewellery

MEERSCHAUM Very light porous soft stone, used to make pipes, also made into jewellery including carved beads, in Turkey and Tanzania

MELON BEAD Common bead shape, round with longitudinal grooves giving segmented appearance.

MELON SEED Dried seed easy to pierce with a needle. One fruit provides enough for several long necklaces.

METAL Confusing glassmaker's term for raw glass

METALLIC Sometimes a lustre coating on glass is intense enough to give a metallic effect, such as gold, copper, bronze or gunmetal (which closely resembles the natural stone haematite)

MEXICO The pre-Columbian civilisations particularly valued their natural jade and gold which were

fashioned into large splendid beads and ornaments

MICRO BEAD The smallest glass rocaille or embroidery bead, used in beadwork and embroidery. No longer imported into Britain from Czechoslovakia but still made and available from US importers.

MILAGROS Latin American metal 'votive offering' charms (Guatemala, Mexico, etc.)

MILLEFIORI Thousand flowers. General term; popular ancient to present-day method of decorating glass beads, used in Roman glass, Viking beads, Venice, Czechoslovakia, Far East and India. Patterns made in 'canes' with decorative cross-section, like seaside rock pulled out long and thin. Flat slices of the pattern are melted onto the surface of cylindrical or round beads on a darker glass core. Otherwise known as chachasao or karakumba.

MOCCASINS North American Indian leather or hide slippers often with charming bead embroidery motifs

MOHS SCALE A measure of hardness of stones measured from 1 to 10, from talc to diamond. Glass is

Necklaces with old cornelians.
From outside: 'bar of soap' cornelian, meerschaum from Tanzania, African-type amber, with braided ends. Round cornelians, tropical nuts (Indian rudraksha from Java) with metal and spotted trade beads. Old Indian 'date'-shaped cornelians from Africa, with brass beads. Old Tibetan cornelians with two metal filigree beads

around 5 to 6.

MONKEY BONE Bone beads from Nigeria are described as monkey bone, often decorated with inscribed dot and circle eye pattern

MONKEY'S FIST Useful neat round knot

MONOFILAMENT FISHING LINE Single filament gut rather than spun yarn used for threading, rather stiff

MOONSTONE Translucent semi-precious stone with lustrous milky shimmer

MOSAIC See millefiori

MOSS AGATE Translucent agate with veins resembling green vegetation

MOSSI BEAD Tribal name for biconical glass bead with rough facets and conical hole. Often vaseline glass (q.v.) or transparent or milky light green or pale Wedgwood blue. Traded by Dutch or Portuguese but most likely Czech (made by a process called dry moulding).
MOTHER-OF-PEARL White pearly oyster shell which is easily carved into beads and pendants; currently a tourist market for rosaries of mother-of-pearl in the Holy Land, also big industry in the Philippines
MOULD-MADE BEAD All sorts of materials are cast in moulds, generally used to produce identical beads in quantity. With Czech glass beads the mould has two halves, and a seam, ridge or line is generally visible where they join, either longitudinal or around the centre.
MUFF CHAIN Extremely long string of beads with fastener to go through and hold a muff (hand warmer)
MULTISTRAND A necklace of two or more strands which join to one clasp, maybe going through multi-strand spacers or graduated
MUMMY BEADS See ceramic
MURANO Island near Venice where glass-making industry has been situated since the thirteenth century
MURRINE DISC Millefiori-slice pendant
MUTISALA Indian red glass seed beads brought from India into Africa
MYRRH Small fragrant beads made of myrrh resin in Mali, Africa

NACRE Substance that forms as mother-of-pearl on side of oyster shell or as a round pearl
NAGA Primitive Himalayan peoples between India, Tibet and Burma with traditional distinctive bead jewellery
NAME BEAD See alphabet bead
NATURAL BEAD Many pips, stones, beans, nuts, seeds, shells, twigs, even pods can be pierced soft or drilled and threaded just as they are
NDEBELE South African tribes with own distinctive beadwork style
NECKLACE Piece of jewellery, generally loop of beads on thread, to hang round neck
NECKLET Diminutive of necklace, perhaps intended to mean short, small, or less extravagant
NECKLET ENDS See bullion
NEEDLE FILE Slender, tapering file of various cross-sections for fine work
NEPHRITE One of the green gemstones known as jade (q.v.)
NETSUKE Japanese bead attaching 'inro' pouch to sash with 'ojime' sliding-bead fastening. These items

are exquisitely made in many materials, highly valued and collected
NOOSE Self-tightening loop or knot, may attach a fastener
NUGGET Crude metal lump, bead or pendant
NUMBER BEAD Similar to alphabet bead
NYLON Continuous multi-filament spun yarn, recommended as strongest thread for beads if available. Can be used many strands together. Usual thickness 40, finer 60, finest 80. Knots very well.
NYLON MONOFILAMENT GUT (fishing line) Stiff, solid, colourless line used for threading; hard to knot

OAK APPLE See natural bead
OBLATE BEAD Short or truncated sphere shape, having a diameter fatter than its length
OBSIDIAN Black semi-precious stone (volcanic rock), sometimes white markings (snowflake obsidian)
ODONTOLITE Turquoise-green substance, actually fossilised bone stained naturally by the presence of copper
OJIME Sliding bead with netsuke and inro
ONYX 1 Onyx marble: soft alabaster, easily carved into beads etc.
2 Name given to black and white banded agate
OP BEADS Old name of large cylindrical trade beads; meaning of initials unknown
OPAL Precious stone with wonderful multicoloured iridescence, only rarely made into beads; difficult to drill
OPALINE Any type of white milky glass with a bluish-orange opalescence when held up to light
OSTRICH EGGSHELL DISC These have been made in Africa since the earliest times, and in other places since

PADRE BEAD Name of a specific old blue wound bead, probably Chinese, traded in America
PAILLETTE Type of larger, flat, stitch-on decorative sequin for embroidery, particularly for clothing
PAINTED BEAD Hand-made decorated glass lamp-work beads are often mistakenly called painted. Beads can be decorated with fine painting but it is liable to wear off in normal use.
PAKEEZA Indian long tubular beads for lampshade fringes, curtains, etc.
PALM NUT Large dhoum palm nut, carved decoratively as beads etc. in Kenya
PANELLED A form of bead with flat panels on the sides
PAPIER MACHÉ Modelling mixture of shredded paper

soaked in gum; tough and light when hard

PAPIER ROULÉ Beads made of rolled up paper triangles

PARURE Set of several matching pieces of jewellery, or one very ornate jewellery item, for example a formal or elaborate necklace arrangement with loops and dangles

PASTE Paste jewellery is glass imitating faceted gemstones but not beads; also known as diamanté or rhinestone.

PATERNOSTER The larger beads on rosaries. *See* chevron.

PATINA A mellow surface texture, the result of age, wear and handling, or artificially created to enhance appearance, particularly on metal

PEACH STONE BEAD The Chinese carve intricate lifelike designs on fruit stones of the peach family, depicting fruit, flowers, butterflies, dragons, people, landscapes, including houses and ships, and the disciples of Buddha

PEAR SHAPE Fairly common bead shape

PEARL Naturally formed inside the pearl oyster, or cultured when the nucleus round which it is formed is artificially inserted inside the oyster and allowed to accumulate layers. Pearls are harvested in pearl farms in the sea or fresh-water lakes, then sorted, graded and drilled and threaded. Most at present come from China, Hong Kong, Japan and India. Real pearls come in a variety of tints from creamy white, pink, gold, blue grey to black. They lose their lustre if they are not handled and worn. Baroque pearls are irregular in shape. Artificial or simulated pearls are glass beads with a coating of pearl varnish. The difference can easily be discerned by rubbing the bead against your tooth: a natural pearl makes a grating sound whereas a varnished glass pearl is smooth and slips over the tooth.

PEARLISED Made to resemble the lustrous effect of the pearl

PEBBLE Can be polished and drilled and used in its natural colour and form as a bead. Cornelian and agate are sometimes found as pebbles.

PECTORAL A large piece or pendant hanging across the chest

PEKING GLASS Glass lampwork beads from China recognisable by their pattern of bubbles, the white clay inside the hole and characteristic colours – strong opaque raspberry pink, transparent olive yellow and beautiful greens and blues

PENDANT General term for a sizeable hanging ornament with hole or loop at the top, worn by itself or as the centre of a necklace, or as drop earrings or one of a number in a threaded pattern

PERFORATION Another word for hole

PERFUMED BEAD Many recipes exist for modelling beads with added fragrant oil which give off their scent when next to a warm body. *See* rose-petal paste.

PERIDOT A light-green transparent semi-precious stone

PETRIFIED WOOD or FOSSILISED WOOD A grained browny jasper that has formed where wood became buried and 'turned to stone'

PEWTER Greyish metal used as sheet and wire in cheaper hand-worked jewellery, late Victorian, Edwardian, arts and crafts, etc.

PEYOTE STITCH Honeycomb beadwork stitch worked spirally to produce a beadwork sausage

PHOENICIAN Pheonician beads are sometimes mis-attributed. The Phoenicians of 300BC onwards mostly traded in other nations' products, though Roman glass 'face' and 'eye' beads were being made in their cities, including Carthage.

PICASSO BEAD Opaque pastel-coloured moulded bead painted with blotchy iridescent coating. Manufacturer's name.

PICOT Term borrowed from tatting and lacemaking for small decorative loops along edges in bead lace etc.

PINCHBECK Victorian alloy in imitation of gold

PINCUSHION Coloured beads on pins were used to create patterns on decorative pincushions, from Victorian era to World War 1 in particular

PIN VICE Small tool which tightens to hold a pin or small tool such as a broacher

PIPE Bugle or larger tubular bead

PIQUÉ Victorian metal-inlaid tortoiseshell beads, earrings and pendants

PLAIT *See* braiding

PLASMA Also known as dark green jasper

PLASTIC Versatile group of man-made materials used for bead production, either moulded for quantity production, cut, welded or formed using heat. Thin sheets can be pressed or vacuum formed, and it can be coated with a plating of metal.

PLIERS Essential gripping and bending tool for many of the jewellery processes involving beads especially on wire, such as round-nosed, snipe-nosed, rosary, chainlink, etc.

PLUMBER'S BEAD Enormous egg-shaped wood bead 15cm (6in) long or more, singly or on a chain in regular sizes. Used by plumbers of bygone times for shaping lead pipes.

POKERWORK Natural pale wood can be decorated into patterns by singeing with a red hot point (pyrography)

POLYCHROME GLASS BEAD Many coloured

POLYESTER A man-made fibre common as sewing thread

POMANDER Small receptacle for aromatic substances,

may be worn as pendant, and to protect from disease

POMPADOUR Term for type of lace bobbin bead

PONY BEAD *See* Congo bead

PORCELAIN 1 Incorrect name for opaque white glass as distinct from real porcelain
2 Real porcelain is moulded, fired at a high temperature and glazed to form beads

PORPHYRY Purply-brown marble

POT BEAD Small African powder glass bead made in Nigeria and Ghana

POTTERY *See* ceramic

POUND BEAD Small bead, rocaille type, sold by weight

POWDER GLASS BEAD West African method of casting beads from ground-up glass (medicine or beer bottles or broken beads). The glass fuses solid without completing melting, so it looks rough.

PRASE *See* chrysoprase

PRAYER BEADS Christian, Muslim, Hindu and Buddhist all use strings of counting beads as an aid in reciting their prayers

PRE-COLUMBIAN Pre-Columbian, Central and South America

PRESS MOULDED Czech method of manufacture, pressing hot glass into moulds like a waffle iron

PRESSED AMBER *See* ambroid

PRIEST BEAD Large grey African powder glass cylinder with longitudinal lines (gashi)

PROCESSIONAL (of necklace) Having a continuous repeating sequence

PROFILE Side view outline with hole vertical

PROSSER MOULDING or DRY MOULDING Another way of moulding glass, particularly beads. Named after inventor.

PURL *See* bullion

PURSE MOULD Victorian beaded purses crocheted

with beads were more easily constructed around a cylindrical wooden purse mould, later slid off and finished

PYRITE (fools' gold) Wrongly called marcasite. Yellow or greyish metallic-looking stone, attractive though rarely made into beads.

PYROGRAPHY *See* poker work

QUARTZ Name covers a large group of semi-precious stones; quartz crystal-clear, smoky quartz – grey, citrine – yellow-brown, rose quartz – pink, amethyst – purple, tiger's eye

QUILL Porcupine quills were cut and used for embroidery by North American Indians before the introduction of glass embroidery beads by traders

RAFFIA A natural plant fibre used for braiding, macramé and threading

RAKU Type of Japanese ceramic technique, producing interesting unexpected surface colours and textures

RAT TAIL Fat shiny round polyester braid in many colours

RECONSTITUTED (turquoise, amber, ivory, etc) Small fragments of chippings of the stone combined with a medium such as resin for an economical version of the same stone

RESIN Natural resin is secreted from certain trees; amber and copal are natural hard resins. Also used as glue or embedding. A modern synthetic resin has many jewellery uses. Only natural resins give off a pleasant fragrance when warmed or burned; mastic is a natural resin.

RHINESTONE American term for diamanté

RHODOCHROSITE Soft raspberry-pink stone with pale visible strata found in Argentina

RHODONITE Pinkish stone with black marks

RIBBON Narrow woven strip or band of fabric (often velvet) used as threading material or as choker, stitched on beads or pendant, or as a tie fastening

---

Carved and curious collectables.

Top left: pre-Columbian Central American carved stone beads.

Below: five 'dzi' beads – ancient etched agates highly valued in Tibet, one with silver collar. At right of pendant is one black and white bead of 'folded glass' probably from early glass bead production in India. Below, two rows of six oval and six round patterned petrified wood beads from Himalayan tribes, possibly eighteenth century.

Bottom left: three modern 'dzi' motif beads from India: carved bone, and decorated glass.

Next vertical row, from top: heads and faces: Chinese and Japanese beads of lacquer, cast metal, pottery, moulded composition, carved bone skulls (Tibetan Buddhist prayer beads).

Next vertical row: Japanese lacquer with mother-of-pearl inlays, carved wood, bone and ivory, ebony, vegetable ivory.

Next on left, loose: four twentieth-century plastic imitation 'dzi' beads, 1920s 'Egyptiana' Pharaoh's head moulded porcelain. String with Czech 1920s scarab, 'Egyptiana' beads, arm and leg Central American votive pendants ('milagros'), modern Middle East folded glass eye bead, millefiori face bead made for trading, millefiori trade bead with the word 'AFRICA' on two sides, possibly Venetian oval glass bead with skull and crossbones.

Last long string: twenty-four Chinese carved oval nuts with Buddhas, dragons, fruit, flowers, butterflies, fish, a crab, monkeys, knots, and a boat full of people

RING Jewellery for finger etc., can be made with bead or beads and wire. Beads can also be ring shaped (annular).

RIVIÈRE Necklace

ROCAILLE Oblate glass seed bead or embroidery bead, 15mm (⅗in) or smaller, made by the drawn glass tube method

ROCK CRYSTAL Natural crystal (clear quartz), not glass

ROD Glass is used in the form of rods or canes for lampwork

RODE Variety of Congo bead

ROLLED GOLD or GOLDFILL A pinkish yellow tough metal with a proportion of fine gold which stays bright. Good for findings and attachments.

ROMAN GLASS Beads were made of glass between 300BC and AD200 mostly Near or Middle East under Roman rule. Various methods of mandrel-wound and trail decoration including millefiori.

RONDELLE Rounded doughnut-shaped disc

ROPE BEAD Tiny Victorian metal bead, rocaille size, with diagonal grooves giving a twisted look. Modern-day crimps resemble them.

ROSARY Christian prayer beads

ROSARY PLIERS Combined round-nosed pliers and cutters

ROSE-PETAL PASTE A compound for modelling fragrant beads

ROSE QUARTZ See quartz

ROSETTA See chevron

ROSETTE Flat rosette-shaped, lateral hole, carved or moulded

ROSEWOOD An attractive wood sometimes carved into beads

ROTELLE Disc-shaped round bead

ROUND-NOSED PLIERS Pliers with tapered smooth conical jaws for bending wire in small loops

RUBBER Plant secretion that can be shaped. Hard rubber (vulcanite) was made into black beads imitating jet. Also red as coral. Gutta-percha seems to be a form of rubber.

RUBY One of the precious stones, deep crimson. Ruby beads are made of the turbid portions of stone (not completely transparent).

RUDRAKSHA A wrinkled dark brown five-sided nut, made into Hindu prayer beads all over India. Grows naturally only in Java.

RUSSIAN BLUE See ambassador bead

RUTILATED QUARTZ Clear quartz with fascinating rod-like inclusions

S LINK S shaped wire link for connecting beads on wire in chain necklaces or earrings

SAFETY CHAIN An additional fastening to protect from loss, connected to each end of a necklace

ST CUTHBERT'S BEADS Small black circular fossil stones found on coast of Northumbria. Supposed to be fossilised vertebrae of dinosaur's tails.

SAMPLE CARD Invaluable as evidence of type, origin, age and place of manufacture, to be preserved as they are

SANDALWOOD Fragrant wood from Far East used for beads

SANDCAST See powder glass

SAPPHIRE Clear blue precious stone

SARD Cornelian

SARDONYX Striped (layered) cornelian

SATIN A satin appearance is achieved either by a matt surface, an effect inside semi-translucent glass, or in tubular beads with elongated air bubbles

SAUTOIR Very long looped necklace, could be worn diagonally (over one shoulder)

SCARAB In ancient Egypt the scarab beetle was specially venerated, representing spiritual rebirth; its compact oval shape, flat underneath, was very common as an amulet or seal; often made of carved glazed steatite or faience. When Tutankhamun's tomb was discovered, which was front page news in the 1920s, it led to the popular Egyptian style and scarabs were profusely made as moulded Czech glass beads among other Egyptian motifs.

SCRABBLE BEAD Name for a haphazard type of trail decoration

SCREW CLASP Simple and common barrel-shaped base metal fastener

SEAL Since ancient times some beads, particularly cylinder and scarab shaped, are made as seals with engraved patterns to imprint their mark

SEALING WAX BEAD Beads can be made or decorated with sealing wax (for example to resemble coral) but they are not very long lasting

SECOND CUT A type of faceted cut embroidery bead with long and diagonal facets

SEED Many seeds are often used as beads, including Job's tears, melon seeds, sunflower seeds, maize kernels, etc.

SEED BEAD Rounded rocaille

SEMI-PRECIOUS All the gemstones except the traditional precious stones

SEQUIN Small glittery or metallic disc to decorate clothing, often used with embroidery beads

SERPENTINE An opaque and variegated green stone

SETRO The ancient Egyptian word for necklace maker

SHASHA Egyptian good-luck beads

SHELL Shells of every type are and have been used as beads and pendants, whole or shaped

SILK Until the development of man-made fibres, the strongest thread for beads was silk

SILVER Precious metal usually alloyed with small proportions of other metals for strength, made into enormous variety of beads by every method, also findings. Laws in England dating back to the fifteenth century control the quality of silver (also gold) by requiring items to conform to certain proportions of the metal in order to be hallmarked, and it is illegal for a trader to sell anything other than small components as 'silver', unless they are hallmarked. Fine silver, standard silver and sterling silver are hallmark quality. Silver made into jewellery in India has too low a percentage of real silver and may only be described as 'native silver'.

SLIDING BEAD Method used on Indian necklaces to tighten or loosen

SLIP KNOT Self-tightening knot useful for attaching fasteners

SMOKY QUARTZ See quartz

SNAKE BEADS Moulded glass zig-zag shapes that fit together when threaded and articulate to resemble a snake. Many types were made in Czechoslovakia for trade in Africa.

SNAP FASTENER See box snap

SNIPE-NOSED PLIERS Pliers with each jaw tapering so that together they close to a point with a flat inner surface

SOAPSTONE Common name for steatite (talc). One of the softest, most easy to carve, stones. Cream, grey, browny-green.

SODA GLASS Glass with low melting point making it easy to use for lampwork

SODALITE A blue semi-precious stone, resembles lapis but with white calcite streaks

SOUVENIR Beads, pendants or charms may be collected as personal or tourist souvenirs especially if their material or form relates to the place, event or thing remembered, such as olive wood from the Holy Land, or miniature replica of the Eiffel Tower, anvil for Gretna Green, shamrock or harp for Ireland, etc. However, souvenirs are often not very well made.

SPACER Bead, panel or strip with parallel holes to keep strands evenly apart, or any small beads, metal, etc. intended to go between important beads

SPANGLE Wire loop with five, seven or nine handmade glass beads at bottom of English lace bobbin; a large 'bottom bead' with pairs of 'square cuts' up the sides

SPANISH GLASS An old type of moulded glass faceted bead, cornelian colour, used for trade; probably named after the beads' traders as they are now thought to have been made in Czechoslovakia

SPINDLE WHORL Resembling large conical or round beads. Ancient and primitive peoples used them as weights when spinning yarn. Usually unglazed ceramic or stone.

SPLIT RING Base metal finding resembling a key-ring. Small ring that a bolt ring attaches to on a necklace. Although not soldered, much more secure than a jump ring.

SQUARE CUT Lacemakers' term for small marvered square lampwork beads for bobbin spangles

SQUIGGLE Type of Venetian lampwork bead decoration

STABILISED (of turquoise) Impregnated with resin to protect and prevent darkening of colour

STAINED AGATE, MOTHER-OF-PEARL, BONE, etc. Agate, jasper and various substances can be stained or the natural colour can be enhanced – as it usually is nowadays

STAMPED Beads of soft material with impressed designs, or sheet metal shaped by stamping (two halves of bead soldered together)

STAR BEAD See chevron

STEATITE See soapstone

STEEL Tiny cut steel beads were used in embroidery and beadwork like rocailles in the Victorian and Edwardian eras

STONE Aside from gemstones, mineral aggregates and rock which can be carved into beads (marble and granite etc.)

STRAND One string of several on multistrand necklace

STRATA Natural layers in gemstone formation

STRAW BEAD Tubular glass bead

SUN STONE Golden-coloured natural aventurine

SWEEPINGS Some bead shops sell bargain mixed bags full of odds and ends of beads called sweepings, which is cheaper for them than spending time sorting them out

SWIRLED Lampwork decoration of random colours swirled together

SWISS LAPIS Grey jasper stained with cobalt (Prussian blue) as substitute for lapis lazuli, but quite an attractive colour

SWIVEL CLASP Small spring clasp, similar to that on a dog's lead, which swivels at its base

SYNTHETIC Artificially made substitute beads, often plastic or glass, to resemble gemstones

TABULAR Any flat bead shape with hole through length so it lies flat (tabular oval, hexagon, etc.)

TAIRONA Pre-Columbian Central American civilisation which made quantities of distinctive beads

TALC See soapstone

'Primitive' necklaces.
From outside: snake vertebrae, pokerwork on wood, teeth and bones, Solomon Islands nut and shell discs and pendant

Two Raksha Mala, Tibetan amulet necklaces

TALISMAN Charm or pendant of magic significance to attract positive forces

TALLY BEADS Counting beads, as on abacus

TAMBOUR BEADING Typing of bead embroidery worked on fabric stretched on a tambour frame using a fine tambour hook, worked from the back of the fabric

TAPE Used for threading (see ribbon)

TASBIAH Muslim prayer beads

TASSEL Bunch of threads, chains or bead strings hanging together decoratively, often on ends of strands or earrings

TAXILA Ancient bead trading centre in northern India

TEETH Like nuts or shells, natural objects that have been used as some of the earliest beads

TEMPERA Opaque paint (pigment plus egg yolk) used to decorate gesso; can be used for polychrome beads if burnished

TENSION Maintain even tension when knotting

TERRACOTTA See ceramic

TERYLENE Man-made fibre used for sewing thread; can be used for beads

THONG Narrow, very strong, leather strip or cord, for example bootlace, used to thread beads with large holes or hang a pendant

THREAD Spun fibre yarn on which beads may be threaded

THRUM Loose offcut of thread. Waste product of weaving, but silk thrums can be useful for creating beautiful braids.

TIARA Rigid jewelled female head ornament; can be made of wire and include beads

TIE A necklace may be fastened with ribbon ties

TIFFANY BEAD Fine quality, spherical, transparent, coloured moulded glass bead; trade name

TIGER TAIL Fine stranded stainless steel cable coated with clear nylon, the strongest threading line but stiff; needs special threading techniques

TIGER'S-EYE Semi-precious stone (member of quartz family); has distinctive gold-yellow-brown satin shimmer effect

TIKI New Zealand green stone (nephrite) lucky pendant

TILE BEAD Regular moulded large-holed short cylindrical opaque bead that looks square from the side. Often used for mats, threaded honeycomb fashion. Also known as cube allies.

TIN CUT Faceting process for type of embroidery bead

TINSEL Metallic strips, threads or flat pieces, used to add glitter in embroidery or for inexpensive ornament

TOGGLE Originally a bar-shaped button with hole half-way along. Useful with buttonhole as fastening. A toggle bead is any long shape with hole half-way, torpedo or dumbell shape, or irregular such as freshwater pearls or coral twigs.

TOMBODAMA Japanese word for bead maker

TOPAZ: Clear precious stone of gold-yellow colour

TORPEDO Characteristic bead shape, elongated convex bicone

TORTOISESHELL Material like horn made popular in nineteenth century as jewellery and ornaments because of beautiful brown markings and ease of working (becomes pliant when heated)

TOSCA Type of transparent embroidery bead with square hole. Its silvered inside gives extra reflections.

TOURMALINE Clear precious stone of several colours: clear, rose, blue, green, brown

TRADE Beads used all over the world for trade and barter, of no special type. Some names refer to the traders rather than place of manufacture, such as Birmingham beads or Spanish glass.

TRAIL DECORATION General technique used in lampwork to apply decoration with molten canes like writing

TRIBAL Another general term either referring to beads made by a particular tribe, for example Krobo, or certain trade beads which were preferred by particular tribes and became associated with tribes' names (e.g. Mossi)

TRIVET Mat on which to put a hot kettle or teapot, sometimes made with tile beads

TRUNCATED When the bead shape appears to have its ends cut off, for instance truncated bicone

TUMBLING Method of polishing beads by rotating in a container with fine abrasive grit and water, or hot tumbling – raw drawn glass beads rotated in a drum near their melting point, so their surface melts and becomes smooth and glossy

TURK'S HEAD KNOT Ornamental knot, sometimes used between beads like a spacer bead, and sometimes knotted independently of other thread and used as a sliding bead on Indian necklaces, in order to open and close them

TURNING Forming while rotating on a lathe – wood, ivory, horn, etc., and even softer stones

TURQUOISE Fragile porous light blue-green precious stone. Chinese, Tibetan, Bedouin and other Islamic jewellery often has a lot of turquoise. Reconstituted turquoise is ground and mixed with resin; stabilised turquoise is impregnated with resin protection.

TURQUORITE Stained howlite

TURRITELLA AGATE Tiny fossil spiral shells embedded in agate

TWEEZERS Watchmaker's tweezers with fine tapered points used for knotting pearls

TWINE Spun or twisted string

TWISTED CHOKER Thick necklace or many strands of small beads twisted around each other to resemble a rope

TZI See dzi bead

ULEXITE Very soft white stone with fibrous satin cat's eye effect

UNAKITE Green and pink swirled serpentine

VASE BEAD Refers to shape; characteristic among Roman glass beads, for instance

VASELINE GLASS A particular almost transparent yellow glass resembling vaseline; see also Mossi bead

VEGETABLE IVORY To keep up with demand for ivory from the Far East, the nut of a Central American palm was used as a substitute, the colour and grain of which is very similar to that of ivory. Beads were carved and stained.

VENETIAN BEAD Glass beads have been made in Murano, Venice, since pre-Renaissance times. These days any finely decorated glass beads that look old tend to be called Venetian, regardless of their origin.

VERMEIL Gold plated on to silver, bronze or copper

VERTEBRAE Fish or snake vertebrae have a central hole and have been strung and used as beads, in Africa for instance

VICTORIAN Jewellery in all forms including beads flourished in Queen Victoria's early reign with the increased prosperity of the Empire and access to colonial resources of precious materials. Designs were derivative but lavish. When Prince Albert died, the Queen made jet and sentimental jewellery popular. The arts and craft movement and art nouveau grew towards the end of the century, and are sometimes confusingly called 'Edwardian'.

WAMPUM Traditional North American Indian tubular shell beads of white and purple, no longer made in quantity

WATER GILDING Traditional method of applying gold leaf on to prepared gesso base, using diluted egg white and finishing by burnishing

WAXING Threads are rubbed with beeswax to strengthen and lubricate them during the threading process

WEDDING CAKE Any ornately decorated wound glass bead with lines left proud like icing on a cake

WHIPPING Smart and durable way to protect and secure a bunch of strands of thread or end cord by winding a thin thread around in an even close spiral

WHITBY Seaside town on Yorkshire coast where best jet was found, especially in Victorian era

WHITE HEARTS See cornaline d'Aleppo

WIRE For threading beads when a rigid structure is desired (chainlinks, earrings, etc.)

WITCH STONE Natural flint pebble with hole, once considered strong magic. If you looked through the hole at someone you would be able to see if they were a witch or not, and perhaps even neutralise their power.

WORRY BEADS Resemble Islamic prayer beads but are just for playing with

WREATH Circle or garland resembling flowers and leaves

WYNBERG BEAD Small even large-holed moulded glass bead; mentioned in 1913 pattern leaflet

XHOSA South African tribe which makes a variety of beadwork jewellery

YORUBA Nigerian tribe with tradition of beadwork decoration on masks, carvings, ceremonial costumes, etc.

ZEBRA JASPER Natural brown and white banding on jasper from southern Africa

ZIG-ZAG BEADS See snake beads

ZODIAC BEADS Necklace of beads of the stone corresponding to a person's birth sign

ZONE Zone decoration, in a band around the centre of the bead

ZULU South African tribe with prolific production of beautiful beadwork. Long and short necklaces, collars, head decoration, belts, purses, aprons, etc. 'Zulu beadwork' is erroneously used to denote native African beadwork in general.

APPENDICES

MUSEUMS AND ANTIQUE MARKETS

Almost every major city in the world has a museum of anthropology, ethnology or national history with representative collections of historic crafts, beads and jewellery, though the beads are not always easy to find and are sometimes confusingly labelled.

Local museums, stately homes and costume collections through the UK are worth investigating. In London there are The British Museum, Victoria and Albert Museum, University College Museum, Horniman Museum, Museum of Mankind and the Commonwealth Institute. The Museum of Archaeology and Ethnography, Cambridge, and the Pitt Rivers Museum, Oxford have outstanding collections of beads and beadwork. York, Sheffield and Whitby have museums with collections of jet jewellery.

Of particular interest are the specialist museums in the manufacturing areas:

Czechoslovakia: Museum of Glass and Bijouterie, Jablonec Nad Nisou
Germany: Schmuck museum, Pforzheim, W Germany
Italy: Museo del Vetro, Murano, Venice
USA: Corning Museum of Glass, Corning, New York; the Bead Museum, Prescott, Arizona

More fun than museums are antique markets, where items can be examined, handled and discussed, although any information should be taken with a pinch of salt. Get there early – successful dealers go home as soon as they have done enough business. Visitors to the UK from the US will find the following London antique markets particularly fascinating:

Collection of bead gadgets and toys.
Clockwise: 'beadwind' for making rolled paper beads; pre-war bead threading set with booklet; 'bead stringer and knot tier;' 'Apache' bead loom with instruction booklet, 1913; pocket bead machine (fill the hopper, turn a handle and jiggle the beads onto a needle with thread coming out at the bottom)

Monday:	Covent Garden
Wednesday:	Camden Passage, Angel, Islington
Friday:	Bermondsey Square, Tower Bridge; Golborne Road and Portobello Road (northern end)
Saturday:	Portobello Road; Camden Passage, Islington; Camden Lock, Camden Town; Church Street and Bell Street, Marylebone
Sunday:	Vallance Road and Cheshire Street, Whitechapel; Camden Lock, Camden Town

USEFUL ADDRESSES

Gemmological Association and Gem Testing Laboratory of Great Britain, 27 Greville Street, London EC1N 8SU tel: 071-404 3334
Goldsmiths Company, Goldsmiths Hall, Foster Lane, London EC2 tel: 071-606 7010
Crafts Council, 44A Pentonville Road, London N1 9BY tel: 071-278 7700
Bead Study Trust, Mrs Flora Westlake, Secretary, Talland, Fullers, Road, Rowledge, Farnham, Surrey GU10 4DF
Society of Jewellery Historians, Department of Medieval and Later Antiquities, The British Museum, London WC1B 3DG
Centre for Bead Research, Peter Francis Jr, Director, 4 Essex Street, Lake Placid, NY 12946, USA
Society of Bead Researchers, PO Box 7304. Eugene, Oregon, Or 97401, USA
Ornament Magazine, Dr Robert K. Liu, Editor, PO Box 2349, San Marcos, Ca 92079, USA
Bead Society of Great Britain, Dr Carole Morris, Membership Secretary, 1 Casburn Lane, Burwell, Cambridgeshire CB5 0ED

ZODIAC STONES

Aries	Red jasper, cornelian
Taurus	Orange cornelian, rose quartz
Gemini	Citrine, tiger's-eye
Cancer	Aventurine, chrysoprase
Leo	Rock crystal, golden quartz
Virgo	Yellow agate, citrine
Libra	Orange citrine, smoky quartz
Scorpio	Deep red cornelian
Sagittarius	Blue quartz, chalcedony
Capricorn	Onyx, cat's eye
Aquarius	Dark blue tiger's-eye, turquoise
Pisces	Amethyst

STONES OF THE MONTH

January	Garnet or rose quartz
February	Amethyst or onyx
March	Aquamarine or red jasper
April	Diamond or rock crystal
May	Emerald or chrysoprase
June	Pearl or moonstone
July	Ruby or cornelian
August	Peridot or aventurine
September	Sapphire or lapis lazuli
October	Opal or tourmaline
November	Topaz or tiger's-eye
December	Turquoise or zircon

COLOUR ASSOCIATIONS

Rose pink	Tenderness, affection
Ruby red	Passion, warmth, devotion, cheerfulness
Orange	Strength, abundance, regeneration
Yellow	Faith, knowledge, honour
Emerald green	Noble spirit, charity, understanding, temperance
Jade green	Power, fortune, justice
Royal blue	Pure love, wisdom, courage
Light blue	Intelligence
Purple	Mystic vision, intuition, chastity
Black	Grief, depth, endurance, protection
White	Purity, peace
Grey	Modesty, obedience
Clear (transparent)	Clairvoyance, truth, fortitude

WEDDING ANNIVERSARIES

British		American	
1st	Cotton	1st	Paper
2nd	Paper	2nd	Cotton
3rd	Leather	3rd	Leather
4th	Wood	4th	Fruit, flowers, silk
7th	Wool	5th	Wood
10th	Tin	6th	Sugar, candy, iron
12th	Silk	7th	Wool or copper
15th	Crystal	8th	Bronze or pottery
20th	China	9th	Willow or pottery
25th	Silver	10th	Tin or aluminium
30th	Pearl	11th	Steel
40th	Ruby	12th	Silk or linen
50th	Gold	13th	Lace
60th		14th	Ivory
and	Diamond	15th	Crystal
70th		20th	China
		25th	Silver
		30th	Pearl
		35th	Coral/platinum
		40th	Ruby
		45th	Sapphire
		50th	Gold
		55th	Emerald
		60th	
		and	Diamond
		70th	

BIBLIOGRAPHY

Aldred, C. *Jewels of the Pharaohs* Thames and Hudson (1971)

Ashley, C. W. *The Ashley Book of Knots* Faber (1977)

Beck, H. *The Classification and Nomenclature of Beads and Pendants* Shumway, USA (1981)

Carey, M. *Beads and Beadwork of East and South Africa* Shire Ethnography (1986)

Clabburn, P. *Beadwork* Shire Albums (1980)

Davis, M. and G. Pack *Mexican Jewelry* Austin, University of Texas, USA (1963)

Dubin, L. S. *History of Beads* Thames and Hudson (1987)

Edwards, J. *Bead Embroidery* Batsford (1966)

Elliot, A. *Magic World of the Xhosa* Collins (1970)
— *Sons of Zulu* Collins (1978)

Erikson, J. M. *The Universal Bead* Norton, USA (1979)

Fagg, W. *Yoruba Beadwork* Lund Humphries (1981)

Filstrup, C. and J. *Beadazzled* Warne (1982)

Fisch, A. M. *Textile Techniques in Metal* Van Nostrand Rheinhold, USA (1975)

Fisher, A. *Africa Adorned* Collins (1984)

Fournier, R. *Illustrated Dictionary of Practical Pottery* Van Nostrand Reinhold (1977)

Francis, P. *Dictionary of Bead Terms* Center for Bead Research, USA (1979)

Fraquet, H. *Amber* Butterworth (1987)

Gerlach, *Primitive and Folk Jewelry* Dover (1971)

Gill, A. *Beadwork* Batsford (1976)

Grossert, J. W. *Zulu Crafts* Shuter and Shooter, South Africa (1978)

Guido, M. *Glass Beads of the Prehistoric and Roman Periods* Thames and Hudson (1978)

Higgins, R. A. *Greek and Roman Jewellery* Methuen (1961)

Holm, E. *Glasperlen* Callwey, Munich (1984)

Lane, M. *Maggie Lane's Book of Beads* Scribner, USA (1979)

Lewis, P. and E. *Peoples of the Golden Triangle* Thames and Hudson (1984)

Littlejohns, I. B. *Beadcraft* Pitman (1930)

Martin, C. *Kumihimo – Japanese Silk Braiding Techniques* Old Hall Press, Herefordshire (1986)

Maxwell-Hyslop, K. R. *Western Asiatic Jewellery* Methuen (1971)

Muller, H. *Jet Jewellery and Ornaments* Shire Albums (1980)

Ogden, J. *Jewellery of the Ancient World* Trefoil Books (1982)

Orchard, J. *Beads and Beadwork of the American Indian* Museum of the American Indian, NY, USA (1975)

Oved, S. *The Book of Necklaces* Arthur Barker (1953)

Ross, H. C. *Bedouin Jewellery in Saudi Arabia* Stacey International (1978)

Schumann, W. *Gemstones of the World* N.A.G. Press (1977)

Seyd, M. *Introducing Beads* Batsford (1973)

van der Sleen, W. G. N. *A Handbook on Beads* Librairie Halbart, Liège Belgium (1973)

Springett, C. and D. *Spangles and Superstitions* Springett, Rugby (1988)

Wasley, R. and E. Harris, *Bead Design* George Allen and Unwin (1970)

White, M. *How to do Beadwork* Dover (1972)

Whiting, G. *Old-time Tools and Toys of Needlework* Dover (1971)

Wilkins, E. *The Rose Garden Game* Gollancz (1969)

Wilkinson, A. *Ancient Egyptian Jewellery* Methuen (1971)

INDEX

Page numbers in *italic* refer to colour illustrations

Venetian millefiori and lampwork trade beads, majority nineteenth century.
From outside: cylindrical trail-decorated eye beads; blue trail-decorated trade beads; black trail-decorated trade beads; combed decorated and pointed twist-shape beads; ornate goldstone glass, rosebud, and 'latticino' spiral-decorated beads; millefiori cylinders of various types; a large flattened millefiori oval

Acknowledgements and thanks begin with my mum, my grandmothers and great aunts without whose amazing collections of decorated glass beads entrusted to me as a small child and treasured greatly, there might never have been this direction to my work. My friend and collaborator Mary Seyd who sadly died just when we were planning work together on a new and more ambitious volume about the history of beads. Mary wrote *Introducing Beads* (1973); through her, many contacts were established, including writing and lecturing opportunities, and she introduced me to the American periodical *Ornament* which has been an invaluable source of information and inspiration, and through which other contacts and friendships have developed; Mr Peter Francis who checked some of the factual information. Ms Pan Henry who owned the Casson Gallery, whose encouragement, criticism and infallible taste has been a continuous influence and support, and my friend and business assistant Marion Bloch, who didn't know what she was letting herself in for, but has lived through every inch of it. The directions are clear only because Marion fought to simplify the text wherever possible, and often had to crawl under furniture to rescue spilt jarfuls of beads as well. My son and daughter Tom and Miriam who kept the household in cheerful equilibrium whenever I was writing. Jo Pound for the loan of four beadwork chokers illustrated on page 59.

The author would be pleased to hear from collectors and designers interested in joining the Bead Society of Great Britain, which is affiliated to over a dozen international Bead Societies. Please write c/o Necklace Maker Workshop, 259 Portobello Road, London W11 1LR.